IGNITE
YOUR
SPIRITUAL GIFTS
THE BLUEPRINT FOR A SUPERNATURAL MINISTRY

Joe Prado

Ignite Your Spiritual Gifts
© 2025 by Joe Prado
All rights reserved. No part of this publication may be reproduced, stored in a retrieval
system, or transmitted in any form or by any means—electronic, mechanical, photocopying,
recording, or otherwise—without prior written permission of the publisher, except for brief
quotations in printed reviews or articles.

Published by Joe Prado Ministries
East Palo Alto, California

ISBN 979-8-9936247-0-9 (paperback)

Scripture quotations marked NKJV are taken from the New King James Version®.
Copyright © 1982 by Thomas Nelson. Used by permission.
All rights reserved.
Scripture quotations marked KJV are from the King James Version of the Bible.

Printed in the United States of America

To my wife, Patty:
Your faithful prayers, and steady love have carried me.
Thank you for walking with me through every season.

To my children Janelle, Joseph, Tim and their spouses
(Tim, Jackie and Lydia):
Thank you for pushing me to write this book.

CONTENTS

INTRODUCTION
A Personal Invitation 1

CHAPTER 1
Understanding the Spirit Realm 5

CHAPTER 2
The Fivefold Ministry 26

CHAPTER 3
The Prophetic - God's Voice to the Church 48

CHAPTER 4
The Gifts of Revelation 69

CHAPTER 5
The Gifts of Power 87

CHAPTER 6
The Vocal Gifts 100

CHAPTER 7
Spiritual Impartation and Growth 120

CHAPTER 8
The Fruit of the Spirit 140

CHAPTER 9
The Urgent Call 146

INTRODUCTION

A Personal Invitation

Have you ever wondered if there's more to God than what you've experienced? Maybe you've had moments in prayer or worship when something stirred deep inside—an unexpected peace, a whisper that wasn't your own thoughts, a feeling that God was *near*. You paused and thought: *Did God just speak to me?* You're not imagining things. You're being invited. Because yes, there *is* more.

Too many believers love God but live disconnected from the power they read about in Scripture. Healing, prophecy, discernment, and boldness sound amazing, but often feel out of reach. Only reserved for the "special" ones. The spiritual elite.

Here's what I've learned: That power is not exclusive. It's essential. If you've been filled with the Holy Spirit, it's already inside you. The same Spirit that raised Jesus from the dead now lives in you—not just so you can feel His presence, but so you can function in His power. You were never meant to settle for a life of religious routine. You were called to *walk in the supernatural*.

So why does it feel like so few believers actually do? Because most of us were never taught *how*. That's what this book is about—*activation*. We're crossing the threshold now. From casual belief to empowered living. From sitting on the sidelines to stepping into your God-given authority. You don't need another church service. You need a *divine awakening*.

If you've ever said, *"I know there's more"*—you're right. Let's unlock it together.

My Testimony

I didn't start behind a pulpit. I started on the cold floor of a jail cell—broken, bound, and desperate. I grew up in the streets of Compton, California. My parents were in church, but I was running from God. I was caught up in drugs, gangs, and darkness. Until one day, locked up and at rock bottom, I cried out to God. And He came. No choir. No preacher. Just the raw presence of God filling a jail cell. I sobered up in a moment, got baptized in Jesus Name, and was filled with the Holy Spirit, and from that day forward, the supernatural became real. I began hearing His voice, seeing His hand. Walking into rooms where the atmosphere would shift. I wasn't chasing ministry. I was chasing Jesus—and He started to move in me. My weakness became His strength.

Now, 45 years later, I've seen miracles on nearly every continent. But the biggest miracle of all? That He would use someone like me. If He did it for me—He can do it for you.

The Urgency of the Gifts of the Spirit

Look around. These are not normal times. Our cities are breaking under the weight of addiction, anxiety, confusion, and chaos. People don't need another inspirational quote. They need a real encounter with the living God and the only way the Church will rise to this hour is by walking in the power of the Holy Spirit. That means not just surviving—but demonstrating.

The gifts of the Spirit are not optional extras. They are essential tools for every believer: word of wisdom, word of knowledge, faith, gifts of healings, working of miracles, prophecy, discerning of spirits, different kinds of tongues, and interpretation of tongues.

We are not just the Church of sermons—we are the Church of *power*. The same Spirit that filled the upper room still fills us today. However, the gifts don't activate automatically. They require hunger. They require surrender. They require you to *say "yes"*. I didn't write this book just for inspiration. I wrote this book for activation, because this is not theory. We are in a spiritual battle and this is *war*. And we need every soldier equipped.

What You're Holding

Before we go any further, let me be clear: This book isn't a study guide. It's a *roadmap*. There are plenty of books that will give you word studies, doctrinal charts, or theological debates. And that's fine—but this isn't a classroom. This is an *upper room*. It's for people who are tired of waiting to be used and ready to step into their calling. God has already filled you. Already gifted you. He's just waiting on your *yes*.

Some chapters will teach. Some will stir. Others will challenge. You may even feel frustrated at times—and that's okay. Growth always feels like tension before it becomes movement. You'll feel those moments where something tugs at your heart—where the Spirit whispers, *this is for you*. Don't brush it off. That's not emotion. That's *invitation*.

By the end of this book, I don't want you to just *understand* the gifts of the Spirit. I want you to *walk* in them. To *move* in them. To *release* them.

So, before we turn the page, I have one question for you: Are you ready to be used by God? If the answer is *yes*, then welcome. You're about to unlock what's been inside you all along.

CHAPTER 1

Understanding the Spirit Realm

The Visible and Invisible

It's important to understand that there are two realms—two dimensions—that are closer to each other than you might think. What separates these realms isn't distance. It's discernment.

We know the natural realm—it's the world we see, touch, and move through every day. You woke up this morning in the natural. You brushed your teeth, tied your shoes, looked at your phone—that means you've mastered the natural realm. But then there's the spiritual realm. The invisible. The eternal. And make no mistake—it's more real than what you can see with your eyes. In fact, the Bible tells us in Colossians 1:16 that God created both realms, "things in heaven and on earth, visible and invisible" (New King James Version).

Two realms. Side by side. The problem is that most people are only aware of one. But we were actually designed to walk in both. This is where the Gifts of the Spirit operate. Not in the natural. Not in our emotions, but in the invisible. This is why the Gifts of the Spirit are often misunderstood. Because you can't operate them with your physical senses. You can't pick up a prophecy with your physical ears. You can't discern spirits with your physical eyes. You can't lay hands on the sick and see healing if you're only used to moving in the flesh.

You have to be connected to the invisible. Let me say it plainly: If you're only living in the natural realm, you will miss the supernatural power that God wants to release through you. You'll attend church but never walk in power. You'll pray but never break through. You'll hear sermons but never hear God. But once your spiritual senses open—everything changes.

Just like your physical body has five senses, your spirit man also has five senses. You can see in the Spirit. Hear in the Spirit. Feel, taste, and smell in the Spirit. The psalmist said, "Oh, taste and see that the Lord is good" (Ps. 34:8). You're not just meant to learn about God—you're meant to experience Him.

I remember stepping off a plane once, flying into a city where I was going to preach. The moment I got off the plane, I heard a voice in my spirit that was cold and dark. It said, "We know you're here." At first, I thought, what was that? Then the Holy Ghost spoke to me and said, "The principality of this region just acknowledged your arrival."

That's how real the spirit realm is. That's how close it is. When you carry authority in the Holy Ghost, even the enemy takes notice. You weren't meant to live only by what you physically see. You were meant to walk in what is unseen.

This book—this journey—is about learning to operate in the realm you were born for. Because here's what many Spirit-filled believers don't realize: The Holy Ghost didn't just come to dwell in you so you could feel something. The Holy Ghost empowers you to *function* in the supernatural. You've been filled, but have you stepped into the supernatural?

That's what this book is about. Helping you see what's always been within reach, and teaching you how to walk in it.

The Fall of Man Caused the Separation

In the beginning, there was no divide. When God created Adam and Eve, they lived in perfect union with the invisible realm. They didn't just believe in God, they walked with Him. They heard His voice. Genesis 3:8 says, "And they heard the voice of the Lord God walking in the garden in the cool of the day." They were so in tune with the Spirit that they recognized the sound of God's presence moving. There was no confusion, no spiritual guessing game. They lived with full awareness of both the natural and the spiritual. That was normal. That was life as God intended it.

That's what walking in the Spirit is supposed to look like—being led by His Spirit, aware of His presence, and sensitive to His voice. Everything changed when sin entered the picture. Isaiah 59:2 says, "But your iniquities have separated you from your God; And your sins have hidden His face from you, So that He will not hear." The fracture didn't begin with eating the fruit, it began with a question: "Did God really say…?" The serpent didn't come with force; he came with confusion. He twisted what God had said, and Eve listened. She entered a conversation with deception instead of standing firm on the word God had spoken. That hesitation opened the door to everything that followed.

This is why knowing the Word of God is essential for anyone who wants to operate in the Gifts of the Spirit. Every gift—every prophecy, word of knowledge, or discernment of spirits—must be grounded in the Word. If Eve had responded with truth, the serpent's lie would have had no power. That's exactly what Jesus did when He was tempted in the wilderness: He answered every lie with "It is written" (Matt. 4:4). That's how you guard your heart.

Eve had questions, but she didn't consult Adam, her spiritual covering. She made a spiritual decision in isolation, and it led to deception. In disobedience, Adam and Eve's natural eyes were opened, but their spiritual eyes became closed to God's presence. What had once been normal, the presence of God, the clarity of His voice, was suddenly distant. They went from walking with God to hiding from Him. From intimacy to shame. From spiritual clarity to confusion.

Sin always does that. It disconnects us from God, clouds our discernment, and creates distance between us and the realm we were designed to live in. From that moment on, humanity became more comfortable in the natural than in the spiritual. But God, in His mercy, introduced a temporary system to help restore relationships—a way for the sinful man to draw near to a holy God: the tabernacle, the priesthood, and the sacrifices.

Inside the tabernacle was a veil—a thick curtain that separated the Holy Place from the Most Holy Place, the place where God's presence dwelled. No one could enter except the high priest, and only once a year. That veil wasn't just fabric. It was a barrier. A reminder that access had been lost. Thank God, the story doesn't end there. A day was coming when that veil would be torn. And when it was torn, everything changed.

Jesus Restored the Connection Through the Cross

The veil was a constant reminder: the presence of God was close, but not yet accessible. It stood between what was and what could be, a boundary that protected but also restricted. Only the high priest could enter, and only once a year, with blood. It was sacred, but it was limited. Then came Jesus.

Hebrews 10:19–20 says,

> "Therefore, brethren, having boldness to enter the Holiest by the blood of Jesus, by a new and living way which He consecrated for us, through the veil, that is, His flesh."

We know that when Jesus died on the cross the veil in the temple was torn—not from bottom to top, but from top to bottom (Matthew 27:51). God Himself tore it. The barrier was removed. The separation ended. What Adam lost in the garden (intimacy, clarity, and access) was restored through the blood of Jesus.

Jesus didn't just come to forgive sin. He came to give us access. He didn't just come to rescue us from death—He came to reconnect us to life in the Spirit. Through His death and resurrection, He opened the way back into the invisible realm. The door to the supernatural was unlocked, not for a select few, but for every Spirit-filled believer.

We no longer have to wait outside the veil, hoping for a glimpse of God's presence. We've been invited into the Holiest Place. We can walk in the Spirit again. We can hear His voice again. We can operate in the gifts of the Spirit, not in fear, but in boldness, because of what Jesus accomplished at Calvary.

Everything changed at the cross. And because of Jesus, the realm that once felt distant is now our daily reality. Because of Jesus, what was once reserved for the holiest of men is now available to the humblest of believers. The Spirit that hovered over the waters in Genesis now dwells within us. The presence that once stayed behind the veil now flows through the Body of Christ. The realm that was once closed off to humanity has been opened again, not just for visitation, but for habitation. This is the realm where the Gifts of the Spirit operate. This is the realm you were born to walk in.

Spirit, Soul, and Body

Understanding How God Communicates with Us

So now that access has been restored, the question becomes: *How do we access it?* Jesus opened the way, but too many believers are still living as if the veil remains—disconnected, unsure, and spiritually numb. Why? Because even though the Spirit has been poured out, many don't know how to walk in it.

To truly operate in the gifts of the Spirit, we have to understand how God communicates. In order to do that, we need to understand how He created us: not just as physical beings, but as spiritual beings.

You are a threefold being. You are made of body, soul, and spirit. Your body is your physical shell, your senses, your muscles, your brain, your bones. It's the part of you that gets hungry, gets tired, and eventually goes back to the dust.

Your soul is where your personality lives, it includes your mind, your emotions, your memories, your decisions. The soul is eternal; it's the seat of your will and the battlefield for your choices.

But then there's your spirit, the deepest part of you. It's what God breathed into Adam in the garden. It's what died when sin entered the world. And it's what comes alive again when you're filled with the Holy Spirit. Your spirit is your point of connection with God. It's the antenna that receives His signal. It's the part of you that can truly discern, hear, and respond to the voice of the Holy Spirit. This is why *1 Corinthians 2:14* says:

> "But the natural man does not receive the things of the Spirit of God, for they are foolishness to him; nor can he know them, because they are spiritually discerned."

If you're trying to operate in the gifts of the Spirit with just your mind, your logic, or your feelings, it won't work. Why? Because the things of the Spirit are not emotionally felt or intellectually figured out, rather they are spiritually discerned. This is the biggest mistake many believers make. They try to hear God with their feelings. They try to obey Him based on what seems right in their soul. God does not speak through your emotions—He speaks Spirit to spirit.

The soul never sleeps. Even when your body is asleep and your mind is quiet, your spirit remains alert. That is why you can have prophetic dreams. You can feel burdened in your spirit before anything happens in the natural. Your spirit is tuned to a realm that's invisible—but more real than what you can see.

The more you grow in the Spirit, the more you'll begin to recognize when God is speaking and when He's not. You'll stop second-guessing yourself. You'll stop chasing confirmation. You'll start to walk with confidence, not because of what you feel, but because of what you know deep in your spirit.

Operating in the gifts of the Spirit requires this kind of awareness. You can't flow in the prophetic if you're stuck in your emotions. You can't discern spirits if you're only relying on logic. You have to learn how to live and listen from your spirit, because the Spirit of God speaks to the spirit of man and that's where the gifts begin.

God Communicates Spirit-to-spirit

Learning to Hear, Discern, and Respond to the Spirit

Spiritual sensitivity isn't automatic. Just because you've received the Holy Ghost doesn't mean you've automatically trained your spirit to hear clearly. Sensitivity has to be cultivated—just like muscles are built in the gym, and just like musicians train their ears to pick up pitch and tone, your spirit needs to be developed through intentional time in the presence of God.

Some people wonder, *Why don't I hear God clearly?* The question isn't whether God is speaking. God is always speaking. The real question is: *Are you tuned in?*

Think about it like a radio. The signal is always being broadcast but if you're off by even a little, all you'll hear is static. Your spirit needs to be dialed in to the same frequency as the Holy Spirit. That's what sensitivity is. Sensitivity doesn't come by accident—it comes by prayer, by fasting, by worship, and by consistently soaking in the Word.

This is why prayer can't just be one-sided. If all you do is talk, but never wait, never listen, then your spirit will stay dull. We're not just called to talk to God; we're called to commune with Him. And communion means learning to pause, to sit, to wait and let your inner man be trained to recognize the voice of the Holy Spirit.

Spiritual sensitivity also grows through obedience. This is key! Every time you respond to a small prompting of the Holy Spirit—even if it doesn't make full sense to your mind—you're strengthening your spirit's ability to hear and obey. The more you ignore those small impressions, the quieter they get. But the more you respond, the clearer they become. It's not that God stops speaking (remember God is always speaking)—it's that your spirit becomes desensitized when you ignore Him.

Remember, the Gifts of the Spirit don't operate from the outside in. They flow from the inside out. So, if you're waiting to feel something externally before you act, you might miss what God is doing internally. That's why Scripture warns in 1 Thessalonians 5:19: "Do not quench the Spirit."

How do we quench the Spirit? By ignoring Him. By hesitating when He prompts us or by second-guessing what we know in our spirit is right. Over time, that hesitation becomes a habit and that habit becomes a hindrance. But the opposite is also true. When you make it a habit to obey those inner leadings—to speak when He says speak, to lay hands when He prompts you, to pray when you feel the burden—your sensitivity grows. As your sensitivity grows, so does your confidence. As your confidence grows, the gifts begin to flow.

So don't wait for a spotlight moment. Start with stillness. Start with silence. Start by saying, "Speak, Lord—Your servant is listening." God is speaking and He is waiting for someone whose spirit is tuned in enough to hear.

Before you move on, ask the Lord to make your spirit more aware. To quiet the noise. To sharpen your hearing. Because the gifts of the Spirit don't begin with power—they begin with sensitivity.

Hearing the Voice of God
Learning to Recognize and Respond to the Spirit's Leading

So many believers wonder, *How do I know when God is speaking?* And the answer isn't as mystical as people think. God speaks all the time. However, His voice isn't always loud. It's not always emotional or verbal. He speaks through impressions, through peace, unrest, Scripture, people, silence, and through sudden clarity that comes in the middle of a foggy situation.

In John 10:27, Jesus said, "My sheep hear My voice, and I know them, and they follow Me." That means the ability to hear His voice isn't reserved for prophets or preachers. It's for every disciple. Jesus didn't say, *My ministers hear My voice.* He said, *My sheep.* If you belong to Him, you can hear Him.

Here's the issue: most people are listening with the wrong part of themselves. They expect to hear God with their emotions. Or they try to reason their way into discernment. But like we said in the last chapter—God is Spirit, and He speaks Spirit to spirit.

And here's something you need to understand: God speaks with a silent voice. It's not a voice you hear with your natural ears—it's a knowing in your spirit. A sudden clarity. A moment of peace that makes no sense. A check in your spirit that stops you before you go further. It's subtle, but once you learn to recognize it, you'll start noticing He's been speaking all along.

Spiritual Senses: Sight, Hearing, Taste, Touch and Smell

Just like your physical body has five senses, sight, hearing, taste, touch, and smell, your spirit does too. That may sound strange at first, but it's all over Scripture. Psalm 34:8 says, "Oh, taste and see that the Lord is good." Jesus said in Matthew 13:16, "Blessed are your eyes for they see, and your ears for they hear." He wasn't talking about physical sight. He was talking about spiritual perception.

The spiritual realm has textures. It has tones. It has movements. And the more sensitive your spirit becomes, the more you begin to pick up on what God is doing, even when nothing seems to be happening in the natural.

Sometimes you **see** something in the Spirit—not with your physical eyes, but as a picture or vision in your mind's eye. It might be a flash of an image during prayer, or a mental "scene" that drops into your spirit while someone is speaking. That's not imagination, it's revelation.

We see this clearly in 2 Kings 6, when the servant of Elisha panicked because their city was surrounded by an enemy army. From the natural realm, it looked hopeless. Yet, Elisha wasn't shaken. He said, "Do not fear, for those who are with us are more than those who are with them" (2 Kgs. 6:16). And then he prayed, "Lord, I pray, open his eyes that he may see" (2 Kgs. 6:17)
The Bible says,

> "Then the Lord opened the eyes of the young man, and he saw. And behold, the mountain was full of horses and chariots of fire all around Elisha." (*2 Kings 6:17*)

The army had always been there—but the servant couldn't see it until his spiritual eyes were opened. That's how it is with us. God is already moving. His power is already present. The question is, *are your eyes open to see it?*

Then there's **hearing**—the most misunderstood spiritual sense. People expect to hear God like a loud voice in a room, but that's not usually how He speaks. God's voice is silent, but clear. It doesn't sound like thunder. It sounds like peace. It's not always a sentence—sometimes it's a word, a name, a nudge, or a phrase that won't leave you. You might suddenly **feel** prompted to call someone. Or find yourself praying for something you hadn't thought of. Or you're in worship and you hear a word in your spirit that's not from your mind and it aligns with the atmosphere of what God is doing. That's the Spirit speaking.

This kind of sensitivity should be *normal* for Spirit-filled believers—but only if we learn to pay attention to it. The challenge is that we live in a noisy world. A distracted world. And if you don't slow down, you'll miss the subtle ways God speaks. Elijah didn't hear God in the wind, or in the fire, he heard Him in a still small voice (1 Kings 19:12). That has not changed.

God still speaks that way. Quiet. Clear. Personal. Let's be clear—these spiritual senses must always be tested by Scripture. Just because something feels spiritual doesn't mean it's from God. We don't build doctrine on impressions or visions. The Word is the standard. If a prompting or a word contradicts the Bible, it's not from the Holy Spirit. The Spirit of God will never lead you outside the truth of God. Sensitivity is powerful, but it must be grounded in God's Word.

What Gets in the Way?

Recognizing and Removing Barriers to Spiritual Flow

God is always speaking. The Spirit is always moving. If that's true, why do so many Spirit-filled believers feel stuck? Why do people who once burned with passion now feel numb? Why do people with calling and gifting feel blocked, hesitant, or spiritually dry? The answer isn't that God changed. The answer is that something is getting in the way.

When you're filled with the Holy Ghost, the power is already in you. The potential is there. The authority is there. But like a pipe that's clogged with buildup, the flow can be hindered. You can be filled, but still not flowing. That is what this chapter is about—removing the blockages. Clearing the pathway. Making room for the flow of the Spirit in your life. Sometimes it's not the enemy holding you back. Instead, it's what you've allowed to stay hidden in your heart.

Let's walk through the most common barriers to spiritual flow and confront them with Scripture and truth.

Unforgiveness

Nothing will clog the flow of the Spirit faster than a heart that refuses to forgive. Jesus made this clear in Mark 11:25:

"And whenever you stand praying, if you have anything against anyone, forgive him, that your Father in heaven may also forgive you your trespasses."

Forgiveness isn't a suggestion; it's a spiritual necessity. Holding onto offense shuts down your sensitivity. Why? Because unforgiveness doesn't just affect your emotions, it pollutes your spirit. And when your spirit is polluted, your discernment gets clouded.

Bitterness is like spiritual static. It distorts the signal of God's voice. You might be trying to move in the gifts, but nothing comes through clearly because you've allowed a grudge to take up residence in your heart.

Forgiveness doesn't mean pretending it didn't hurt. It means choosing to release them, so you can stay free. Your freedom depends on it.

Pride

Pride is a spiritual wall—it blocks grace, blurs vision, and hinders flow. James 4:6 says, "God resists the proud, but gives grace to the humble."

God doesn't just ignore pride. He actively resists it. And if He's resisting you, it doesn't matter how gifted or anointed you are, nothing is going to flow. Pride makes you think you can do it without God. It makes you lean on talent instead of the Spirit. It keeps you from seeking counsel, submitting to leadership, or admitting weakness. And that kind of self-reliance is deadly in the supernatural.

The gifts of the Spirit don't flow through performance; they flow through humility. God uses the humble because they know it's not about them. They make room for Him.

Fear and Insecurity

Fear is paralyzing. It causes hesitation. It makes you overthink, second-guess, and stay silent when the Spirit is prompting you to speak.

2 Timothy 1:7 reminds us: "For God has not given us a spirit of fear, but of power and of love and of a sound mind." Fear is not just an emotion, it's a spirit. It doesn't come from God. The enemy loves to whisper, "What if you're wrong?" or "What if people judge you?" But when you walk in fear, you shut down the very boldness the Holy Spirit wants to give you.

You don't need to be perfect—you just need to be obedient. God isn't looking for flawless vessels. He's looking for willing ones. And courage in the Spirit doesn't mean you don't feel afraid, it means you obey anyway.

Disobedience

This one is straightforward. Disobedience kills spiritual flow. 1 Samuel 15:22 says, "To obey is better than sacrifice." You can fast. You can preach. You can pray for hours, but if you're ignoring what God told you to do, the gifts won't flow freely through you. God is not going to anoint rebellion.

Sometimes the blockage isn't complicated. God gave you a clear instruction, and you didn't obey. Until that's dealt with, there won't be clarity in the next step. Obedience opens the pipeline for power.

Offense and Bitterness

Hebrews 12:15 says,
> "Lest any root of bitterness springing up cause trouble, and by this many become defiled."

Offense is a seed. Bitterness is the root. And when it takes hold, it doesn't just affect you, it spreads to others. It defiles relationships, church unity, and spiritual sensitivity. If you're easily offended, you'll never last in ministry. If you hold grudges, you'll quench the Spirit. If you stay bitter, you'll stop growing.

Let it go. Deal with it before it becomes a stronghold. You can't walk in the gifts with clenched fists. The Spirit flows through clean hands and an open heart.

Spiritual Laziness

The anointing is free, but walking in the gifts requires discipline. Matthew 26:41 says,
> "Watch and pray, lest you enter into temptation. The spirit indeed is willing, but the flesh is weak."

Many people are waiting for a spiritual breakthrough, but they won't spend time in prayer. They want prophetic insight but neglect the Word. They want to operate in power but never cultivate their inner man.

You cannot walk in spiritual authority if your prayer life is on life support. There's no shortcut. No crash course. Flow requires consistency. It's in the secret place that the gifts are stirred. The lazy never tap into it, only the hungry do.

Carnal Mindset

Romans 8:6 says, "For to be carnally minded is death, but to be spiritually minded is life and peace."

If your mind is consumed with the things of the flesh—entertainment, materialism, comparison, gossip—you will not walk in spiritual authority. Carnal thinking dulls spiritual discernment. It keeps you reactive to your surroundings instead of responsive to the Spirit. This doesn't mean you can't enjoy life. But if your appetite is more tuned to Netflix than to Scripture, don't be surprised if you struggle to hear from God.

Set your mind on the things above. Fill your thoughts with truth. Starve the flesh and feed the spirit.

Lack of Surrender

Romans 12:1 urges us,

> "Present your bodies a living sacrifice, holy, acceptable to God, which is your reasonable service."

The Holy Spirit flows through surrendered vessels. Not strong ones. Not perfect ones. Surrendered ones.

If you're holding onto your own plans, your own timeline, or your own image, the gifts of the Spirit won't flow. Why? Because the gifts aren't for your glory, they're for God's. He won't pour His power into someone who's trying to use it for their own platform.

Surrender doesn't mean you have no ambition. It means your ambition is submitted. It means your gifts are laid on the altar. It means you say, "Lord, whatever You want—I'll do it."

Unrepented Sin

Isaiah 59:2 says,

> "Your iniquities have separated you from
> your God; and your sins have hidden His face
> from you, so that He will not hear."

Sin doesn't disqualify you from being loved, but it will block your connection to God. If you've been walking in hidden sin—pornography, addictions, manipulation, dishonesty—it will eventually dry up your spiritual flow. You might still shout and clap. You might still "look" anointed, but on the inside, there's a disconnect.

The good news? Repentance is powerful. Confess it. Turn from it. The blood of Jesus still cleanses. Don't expect the gifts to flow freely while you're entertaining the very things Jesus died to free you from.

No Accountability or Covering

Hebrews 13:17 says,

"Obey those who rule over you, and be submissive, for they watch out for your soul."

There's a reason God placed you in a church. There's a reason He gave you a pastor. Operating in the gifts of the Spirit without accountability is dangerous. It leads to errors. It opens the door to deception. It creates lone wolves who prophesy without testing, and minister without covering.

The more gifted you are, the more covering you need. The safest people in the kingdom are the ones who are submitted. Correction doesn't kill the gift, it sharpens it. Stay under authority. Ask for feedback. Don't just be gifted, be grounded.

Make Room for the Flow

What is getting in your way? As you've read through these blockages, the Holy Spirit may have brought something to your attention. Don't brush it off. Don't rationalize it. Confess it. Surrender it. Let God clean out the spiritual clutter so the gifts can flow again.

You were never meant to be a reservoir that holds back the Spirit—you were meant to be a river. A vessel through whom the supernatural flows freely. When the blockages are removed, the gifts of the Spirit will flow. Let the Spirit do His work in you so He can move powerfully through you.

CHAPTER 2

The Fivefold Ministry

God's Design

Jesus gave the Fivefold Ministry—apostles, prophets, evangelists, pastors, and teachers—as heaven's blueprint to equip and mature His Church (Eph. 4:11–13). These roles are not about titles, but about function and balance. However, for them to operate as God intended, we first need to understand the foundation they stand on: the difference between authority and power.

There's a reason demons trembled in the presence of Jesus. It wasn't just because of His miracles. It was because of His authority. Luke 4:36 says, "What a word this is! For with authority and power He commands the unclean spirits, and they come out." That line reveals something foundational: authority and power are not the same. And if we're going to operate in the gifts of the Spirit, we have to understand the difference.

Authority vs. Power

In Greek, authority is *exousia*—it means the right to rule, jurisdiction, and legal control. It's not about force; it's about legal standing. Think of it like a police officer holding up their hand to stop traffic. They don't have the physical power to stop a car, but they have the authority to make it stop—and that authority is recognized.

Power, on the other hand, is *dunamis*—where we get the word "dynamite." It's the strength, might, or ability to cause change. Power is force. Authority is the right to use that force.

Jesus operated in both. But here's the key: when it comes to casting out demons, healing the sick, or speaking to storms, authority is what commands obedience. Authority speaks, and creation responds.

> "Behold, I give you authority to trample on serpents and scorpions, and over all the power of the enemy" (Luke 10:19).

Why This Matters

Power alone can stir a room, but authority shifts the atmosphere. Authority is what heaven backs. It does not come through hype or charisma, but through relationship.

"He appointed twelve, that they might be with Him… and have authority to cast out demons" (Mark 3:14–15).

Jesus didn't send His disciples out before spending time with them. Their spiritual authority was born out of intimacy. The more you walk with God, the more authority you carry. It's not about talent or titles. Authority is about alignment. That's why some people can shout and even shake people, but the demons don't move because the authority isn't there. Demons don't obey power, they obey authority.

"*Jesus* summoned His twelve disciples and gave them authority over unclean spirits, to cast them out, and to heal every disease and every sickness." (Matt. 10:1, NASB)

In Acts 8, Simon the sorcerer saw the authority and wanted to purchase it, but Peter rebuked him. Why? Because authority can't be bought, it's granted. And it's only granted to those who are under authority themselves.

Jesus Showed Us How This Works

When Jesus calmed the storm in Matthew 8, He didn't release power, He released authority. He rebuked the wind and it obeyed. The Roman centurion understood this perfectly. He told Jesus, "I am a man under authority…

Just say the word, and my servant will be healed" (Matt. 8:8). Jesus marveled at his faith because the centurion recognized kingdom protocol.

The more submitted you are to God's authority, the more authority you carry. "Submit to God. Resist the devil and he will flee from you" (James 4:7 NKJV). It's not just about resisting. It's about submitting first.

Reclaiming What Adam Lost

In the beginning, Adam was given authority over the earth, but when he sinned, he surrendered it to Satan.

"All this authority I will give You…for it has been delivered to me" (Luke 4:6)

At the Cross, Jesus took it back. He disarmed the enemy, triumphed over death, and reclaimed the keys of authority.

"All authority has been given to Me in heaven and on earth" (Matt. 28:18)

Now, as His Body, we carry that delegated authority—not just to live holy lives, but to advance the Kingdom. We're not here to survive. We're here to subdue. That will only happen when we operate in both power and authority.

Final Thought

If you want to walk in spiritual gifts that have lasting impact—healings that hold, deliverance that sticks, prophecy that pierces—you need more than power. You need authority. That will only come from a life of submission, obedience, and intimacy with God.

So don't just seek power. Seek His presence. Don't just desire the gifts. Desire the Giver. Because when you walk in step with Him, the devil recognizes your voice—not because you're loud, but because heaven backs your words.

God's Blueprint for Building His Church

God never meant for His Church to operate by a corporate structure. He meant for it to run on power, but not just power—divine structure, strategy, and order. The Church isn't a business. It's not a denominational brand. It is the Body of Christ, designed to function with clarity and precision. The blueprint wasn't left to chance—God gave us a divine architecture for how His Church should operate.

Ephesians 4:11–13 lays it out clearly:

> "And He Himself gave some to be apostles, some prophets, some evangelists, and some pastors and teachers, for the equipping of the saints for the work of ministry, for the edifying of the body of Christ."

This is what we call the Fivefold Ministry.

The Fivefold Ministry is God's leadership model for the Church. Five distinct ministry gifts—apostles, prophets, evangelists, pastors, and teachers—each carry a unique function but work together to equip and mature the Body of Christ. These aren't ranks. These aren't titles for spiritual celebrities. These are functions. God-given roles with specific assignments to help the Church grow, unify, and walk in fullness. Let's break down each one.

Apostles: The Sent Ones

Apostles are the sent ones. They carry the burden to build, to pioneer, to plant new works, and to establish foundations. They operate with authority—not to dominate people, but to break open spiritual territory and set things in order.

Think of apostles like spiritual architects. They see the blueprint before others see the building. They don't just start churches, they establish movements. They raise up leaders. They push the Church forward into uncharted regions, both geographically and spiritually. Apostles aren't just figureheads. They labor. They contend. They go where others won't go and build what others won't touch. And when true apostles operate under the power of the Spirit, they bring stability to everything around them.

1 Corinthians 3:10 says, "As a wise master builder I have laid the foundation…"

Prophets: The Voice of God to the Church

Prophets are the eyes of the Church. They don't just predict the future, they reveal the heart of God. They hear what heaven is saying and help align the Church to what God is doing.

True prophets aren't spooky, they're scriptural. They carry a burden for purity. For repentance. For clarity in confusing times. They call the Church back to its assignment and sound the alarm when something is off. Their role is not just to give "words"—it's to equip the Church to hear God. When prophets are operating healthily, they stir discernment, raise up intercessors, and confront anything that grieves the Holy Spirit.

> Amos 3:7 says, "Surely the Lord God does nothing unless He reveals His secret to His servants the prophets."

Evangelists: The Soul-Winners

Evangelists are the soul-winners. They carry the fire for the lost. Wherever they go, they stir hunger for salvation, water baptisms, and the infilling of the Holy Ghost. When an evangelist is in the room, there's an urgency. A call to respond. A pull to the altar.

Evangelists aren't just called to preach crusades; they're also called to equip the Church to evangelize. Their job is to break the fear off the average believer. To remind the Church that the harvest is ready and it's time to move. Evangelists carry a contagious faith. They remind us that God still saves. Still delivers. Still draws people by His Spirit. And their fire helps keep the Church from turning inward. 2 Timothy 4:5 says, "…do the work of an evangelist, fulfill your ministry."

Pastors: The Shepherds of the Flock

Pastors are the shepherds. The ones who stay. The ones who care. They walk with people through valleys and victories. They carry the burden to protect the flock, to guard unity, and to nurture growth. A true pastor doesn't just preach on Sundays. They disciple, counsel, and correct. They cry with you. Pray with you. Challenge you to keep growing.

Pastors carry the heartbeat of Jesus for His people. They don't run from the mess—they walk into it with grace and truth. And they play a vital role in keeping the Church healthy and connected. Jeremiah 3:15 says,

> "And I will give you shepherds according to My heart, who will feed you with knowledge and understanding."

Teachers: The Ones Who Establish Foundation

Teachers are the ones who break down the Word with clarity and depth. They carry the burden to guard sound doctrine and reveal the wisdom of Scripture in a way that the Body can apply. Teachers bring depth to the Church. They make the Word digestible. They show how the Bible connects not just to Sunday services, but to everyday life. Their voice keeps the Church from drifting into hype, emotion, or error.

When a teacher is anointed, even complex truths become simple. And when teaching is valued, the Church matures. 2 Timothy 2:15 says,

> "Be diligent to present yourself approved to God, a worker who does not need to be ashamed, rightly dividing the word of truth."

Together They Equip the Body

God never designed the Church to be built on one gift alone. The Fivefold Ministry was never meant to compete—it was meant to complete. Each role carries something essential. When all five are operating, the Body becomes healthy, balanced, and equipped.

The apostle lays the foundation. The prophet keeps the Church aligned. The evangelist keeps the Church reaching. The pastor keeps the Church together. The teacher keeps the Church grounded. This is why Paul said in Ephesians 4:12–13:

> "...for the equipping of the saints for the work of ministry, for the edifying of the body of Christ, till we all come to the unity of the faith and of the knowledge of the Son of God, to a perfect man, to the measure of the stature of the fullness of Christ."

These ministry gifts aren't just titles, they're assignments. They're roles of responsibility. They're part of God's strategy to mature the Church and activate every believer. Because here's the truth: you may not be called to be a pastor, apostle, or prophet, but you are called to be equipped by them.

The Fivefold Ministry prepares the Church to function in the gifts of the Spirit. To move in the supernatural. To walk in maturity and not be "tossed to and fro by every wind of doctrine" (Eph. 4:14).

Without the Fivefold Ministry, gifts get strange. Without the Fivefold Ministry, zeal has no direction. But when the Fivefold Ministry is present and submitted to the Spirit, everything begins to flow in unity. That's the goal: the fullness of Christ. Not just a good church service. Not just solid sermons. *Fullness.*

So, let's ask the hard question: Are we building God's Church around God's pattern? Is your gifting being activated and equipped—or ignored and dormant? Because if God gave the Church apostles, prophets, evangelists, pastors, and teachers, it's not optional. It's a divine design. And when the blueprint is followed, the Church becomes unstoppable.

Every Believer's Ministry

When Jesus filled you with His Spirit, He didn't just give you comfort, He gave you a commission. He didn't just bring you out of darkness, He called you into purpose. That purpose isn't limited to a pulpit, a microphone, or a church title. It's ministry. And it's for every believer.

One of the biggest lies the enemy has sold to the modern Church is that ministry is for the "anointed few"—the pastor, the preacher, the prophet. However, that's not what Scripture teaches. Ministry is not for the elite. It's for the equipped. Ephesians 4:11–12 makes it clear:

> "And He Himself gave some to be apostles, some prophets, some evangelists, and some pastors and teachers, for the equipping of the

saints for the work of ministry, for the edifying of the body of Christ…"

Read that again: *the saints* do *the work* of the ministry. That means you.

The Fivefold Ministry—apostles, prophets, evangelists, pastors, and teachers—are not meant to do all the ministry. They're meant to *equip* you to do it. Their job is to train, activate, and release the Body into its full function. The goal isn't to build a crowd—it's to build a functioning Body.

You Were Made to Move

1 Corinthians 12 paints a vivid picture of what the Body of Christ is supposed to look like. Paul writes that we are many members, hands, feet, eyes, ears, but one Body. And that every part has a function.

What would happen if your natural body operated the way some churches do? One part doing all the work, while the rest just watched. That's not a body, that is a burden. But when every member knows their role—and walks in it—there's life, flow, and power. The prophetic flows. Healing flows. Words of knowledge flow. Evangelism flourishes. Discipleship deepens.

If you're in the Body, you have a purpose. If you're filled with the Spirit, you have power. There is no such thing as a Spirit-filled believer with no assignment. You may be behind the scenes, but there's still oil on your life. Ministry doesn't always look like a platform. It might look like praying with someone in the parking lot. Speaking a word of encouragement at work. Calling a backslider and prophesying restoration. That is ministry.

Ministry Isn't a Title, It's Obedience

Some people spend years waiting to be "released into ministry"—waiting for a moment, a stage, a title. But here's the truth: the moment God filled you with the Holy Ghost, you were released. Mark 16:17–18 says:

> "And these signs will follow those who believe: In My name they will cast out demons; they will speak with new tongues…they will lay hands on the sick, and they will recover."

It doesn't say, "These signs will follow the ordained." It says, "those who believe."

You don't need a microphone to be used. You need obedience. You don't need recognition, you need faith. Because ministry isn't about being seen. It's about being sent. Too many people are waiting for a title, when God is waiting for a *yes*.

You've Been Filled, Now Be Poured Out

The purpose of the infilling is outpouring.

The Holy Ghost isn't just power for you to feel something in church. It's power to be a witness. Power to operate in the gifts of the Spirit. Power to shift the atmosphere. Power to demonstrate Jesus to a hurting world.

God didn't fill you just so you could clap, cry, and go home. He filled you so you could *pour out*. And the more you pour out, the more He fills you again.

Some people say, "I don't know where to start." Start where you are. Don't wait for a conference. Start in your home. Start in your car. Start in your city. Pray for people. Speak the Word. Share your testimony. Listen for the Spirit's prompting—then obey. You don't need permission to be the Church. You already are.

Final Charge: Stop Watching - Start Functioning

The Church was never meant to be a show. It's not a spectator event. It's a movement—a Body—a supernatural force on the earth. That means *you* have a role to play. You're not too young. You're not too broken. You're not too new. If you've been filled with the Holy Ghost, there's power inside you and it's time to use it. You might not feel qualified, but God never calls the qualified. He qualifies the called.

So, stir up what's inside you. Step out. Take the risk. Lay hands. Prophesy. Encourage. Serve. Pray. Move. Because when every believer steps into their ministry, the Church becomes unstoppable.

Clarifying Apostolic Authority

> "The Church was born Apostolic and it must remain Apostolic."

There's been a lot of confusion surrounding the role of Apostles in the modern Church. Some believe Apostles only existed in the New Testament. Others misuse the title for control or celebrity. But if we're going to build according to God's pattern—not tradition, not popularity, but the *pattern*—we need to understand what Apostolic authority really is.

Apostolic authority isn't about hierarchy. It's not about platforms, popularity, or personality cults. It's about *function*. And it's vital.

Are There Apostles Today?

The short answer: yes. The Bible makes a distinction between different types of apostles. First, there were the Apostles of the Lamb—the original twelve who walked with Jesus and were witnesses of His resurrection (see Revelation 21:14). That group is closed. Nobody today qualifies as an Apostle of the Lamb. That role was foundational.

Now, there's a second category: Ascension-gift Apostles—those whom Jesus gave to the Church *after* He ascended. Ephesians 4:11–12 says:

> "And He Himself gave some to be apostles…for the equipping of the saints, for the work of ministry, for the edifying of the body of Christ."

These Apostles were not part of the original twelve. Paul wasn't. Barnabas wasn't. James, the Lord's brother, wasn't. Yet they were all called Apostles in the book of Acts. Why? Because they functioned apostolically. They built. They established. They governed. They raised up leaders and broke open new regions for the gospel.

That calling didn't end with the first century. If the Church still needs pastors, teachers, and evangelists, why would we assume Apostles are no longer necessary? If we believe in the full Fivefold Ministry, we must also believe that *Apostles still exist today.*

What Does an Apostle Do?

Apostles are more than church planters. More than conference speakers. They are master builders—those who carry revelation, authority, and blueprints from God to establish strong, Spirit-led foundations. Paul described it this way:

> "According to the grace of God which was given to me, as a wise master builder I have laid the foundation…" (1 Corinthians 3:10)

Apostles establish order. They set doctrine. They equip the other gifts. They see farther, dig deeper, and push the Church forward. Apostles carry governmental grace, not to control, but to *align*. They know how to recognize other gifts, call them out, and help them mature. They father people in the Spirit. They birth movements, not just moments.

Apostles carry territorial authority. They don't just pastor a church; they shift a region. They sense the principalities. They discern the assignments. They don't just think about the local building—they think about cities, nations, generations.

Apostles carry a burden for the Body, not just for their own ministry. They don't hoard. They release. They don't compete. They complete. They're not insecure about raising others up—in fact, *that's their job*.

Apostolic vs. Authoritarian

Some people have been hurt by leaders who claimed Apostolic authority, but really just wanted control. They demanded loyalty, silenced questions, and ruled with fear. That's not Apostolic, that's manipulative. Let's be clear: *Apostolic* does not mean *abusive*.

True Apostles serve the Church, not themselves. Paul said in 2 Corinthians 10:8:

> "...even if I should boast somewhat more about our authority...which the Lord gave us for edification and not for your destruction..."

Apostolic authority builds people up, it doesn't tear them down. It releases people into function—it doesn't muzzle them. It confronts sin and corrects errors, but it always aims for health, not harm.

So don't throw out Apostolic leadership just because you've seen it abused. Don't reject God's pattern because of someone else's perversion. The enemy loves to twist what's powerful, but the answer to misuse is not disuse—it's the right *use*.

Apostles and the Gifts of the Spirit

One of the clearest signs of a true Apostolic environment is *the flow of the Spirit*. Where Apostles operate, the gifts of the Spirit are stirred. Prophecy flows. Healing flows. Order and boldness come together. Why? Because Apostles know how to *make room* for the supernatural and also *guard* it from chaos.

The Apostolic calls out what's dormant. It activates what's been stuck. It brings clarity where there's been confusion. It doesn't just bless gifts, it builds them.

That's why churches with Apostolic covering tend to grow in depth and flow. There's structure and spontaneity. There's foundation and fire. Apostles help create safe environments where the gifts can operate in power and in order.

Final Charge: Honor the Blueprint

If we want the results of the early Church, we have to return to the model of the early Church. And that model was Apostolic.

Acts 2:42 says the believers "continued steadfastly in the Apostles' doctrine." Not just in fellowship and miracles, but in the doctrine and direction given by apostolic voices. We need that again. We need Apostles who hear from God, love the Church, and build according to heaven's design. We need Apostles who are not in it for applause, but for assignment.

So, honor the blueprint. Don't reject it. Don't resist it. Embrace it. Because when Apostolic authority is present, the Church isn't just inspired—*it's equipped*. And when the Church is equipped, the world gets changed.

The Pastor and the Gifts of the Spirit

If Apostles build the foundation, Pastors keep the house in order. There's a reason Paul included pastors in the Fivefold Ministry. In fact, they're the only office most churches recognize. And while we need apostles, prophets, evangelists, and teachers—*we desperately need pastors* who understand the flow of the Spirit.

Pastors are not just preachers. They are protectors, nurturers, and shepherds of the local church. They walk with people through growth, grief, correction, and calling. In a Spirit-filled environment, they play a critical role in making sure the gifts of the Spirit don't just move, but mature. It's one thing to have a powerful move of God. It's another thing to *sustain* it. That's where the pastor steps in.

Pastors as Teachers, Correctors, and Motivators

A good pastor feeds the flock. That means teaching sound doctrine—week in and week out. They don't just hype people up on Sundays. They break down truth in ways people can live out Monday through Saturday. Their job isn't to impress; it's to equip. Titus 1:9 says pastors must:

> "...hold firmly to the trustworthy message as it has been taught, so that he can encourage others by sound doctrine and refute those who oppose it."

That means a pastor has to know the Word. Not just emotionally, but accurately. They are teachers at heart—and teaching brings stability.

Pastors also correct. They bring alignment when things drift off course. They confront sin. They bring balance when the supernatural becomes disorderly. Paul told Timothy to "Reprove, rebuke, and exhort, with all long-suffering and teaching" (2 Timothy 4:2).

Correction doesn't mean harshness, it means love with clarity. A good pastor doesn't let foolishness fester. They deal with it in the Spirit of gentleness and they lead people back into alignment.

Pastors motivate. They call people higher. They see potential when others see problems. They don't give up on people—they walk with them through the process of growth. A pastoral voice in your life will push you when you're lazy, comfort you when you're hurting, and pull the gift out of you when you're stuck.

Maintaining Order in the Operation of Spiritual Gifts

This part is critical. Gifts must flow in order. And it is the *pastor's job* to guard that flow. 1 Corinthians 14:40 says, "Let all things be done decently and in order."

Too often, churches either lean too far into *control* (where nothing spiritual happens) or too far into *chaos* (where anything goes). Pastors are called to walk the line between *liberty* and *order*. That means sometimes, a pastor has to say, "Not right now" or "That wasn't the right spirit." Or even, "We're going to pause and wait on the Lord." And that doesn't quench the Spirit—*that guards the flow*.

A healthy church culture is one where the gifts are not just allowed but shepherded. Where people are trained in how to hear God, how to test what they're sensing, and how to submit their gift for evaluation. A place where you don't have to be afraid to step out—but you also know that someone is helping you grow in it, not just letting you run wild.

The best kind of prophetic environment is not one where people give "words" unchecked—it's one where gifts are submitted to *spiritual authority*.

Pastors Who Make Room for the Spirit

Not every pastor has to be a prophet, but every pastor *must* make room for the prophetic. Not every pastor will operate in healing or miracles, but every pastor should create space for those gifts to flow. This means making room in your services for altar calls. For response. For waiting on the Spirit. It means not rushing the presence of God to get to announcements. It means trusting the Holy Spirit more than your schedule.

Some of the greatest breakthroughs don't happen during the sermon—they happen during the yielding. The moment when a pastor says, "We're going to pause here. God is doing something."

If you're a pastor reading this: you don't have to be the most anointed voice in the room, but you *do* have to be the most surrendered. Your surrender creates safety for others to step out in faith.

Submitting Spiritual Gifts to Pastoral Authority

This is for every person in the pew: If you want your gift to grow, submit it to your spiritual covering. Too many people try to flow in the gifts *outside* of their local church. They want to operate in prophecy, healing, or deliverance, but they don't want correction, feedback, or accountability.

That's not how the Kingdom works.

Even Paul submitted his revelations to the leaders in Jerusalem. Even Timothy had to receive impartation and instruction from Paul. If you're too gifted to be corrected, you're too immature to be trusted.

The gifts of the Spirit aren't a free-for-all. They're meant to be exercised *within the context of the Body*. The local pastor is the gatekeeper of that context. If they say "wait," then wait. If they say "grow," then grow. If they say, "not yet," trust their discernment. Your gift will thrive in submission, not rebellion.

Final Charge: Pastors are Gatekeepers of Glory

God gave pastors to the Church not just to teach, but to *tend the fire*. To guard the flock from wolves. To discern what's God and what's flesh. To build people, not just build platforms. And when a pastor partners with the Spirit, something powerful happens: the church becomes a *safe place* for supernatural activation.

If you're a pastor, lean into the Holy Spirit like never before. Don't let fear of disorder stop you from making space for power. And if you're under a pastor, honor their covering. Don't bypass them. Don't try to "minister" without permission. That's how gifts get strange. Stay submitted. Stay teachable. Stay in alignment.

When pastors and gifts flow together the Church becomes unstoppable.

CHAPTER 3

The Prophetic - God's Voice to the Church

Three Operations of the Prophetic

If there's one area of the Gifts of the Spirit that draws both hunger and confusion, it's the prophetic. And for good reason, the voice of God is powerful. It brings direction, correction, clarity, and comfort. It can shift the atmosphere of a room and break open the heart of a person in an instant.

However, not everything that is prophetic is the same. There is a distinction between three operations of the prophetic:
1. The Spirit of Prophecy
2. The Gift of Prophecy
3. The Office of the Prophet

Each of these has a different weight, a different function, and a different level of responsibility. Confusion often comes when we blur the lines between them. When you understand the difference, it brings peace, order, and clarity to the prophetic flow. Let's walk through each one.

The Spirit of Prophecy

This is the broadest and most accessible dimension of the prophetic. It's what happens when the atmosphere is charged with the presence of God and, suddenly, people begin to flow in prophecy who don't normally operate in that way.

Revelation 19:10 says, "The testimony of Jesus is the spirit of prophecy." That means when Jesus is lifted up, when the Gospel is being proclaimed, when hearts are burning in worship—the atmosphere becomes ripe for prophetic flow. It's not about the person; it's about the presence. In that type of atmosphere, even someone who doesn't typically move in prophecy may suddenly feel the unction to speak a word from the Lord.

We see this in 1 Samuel 10:10 when Saul came among the prophets, "...the Spirit of God came upon him, and he prophesied among them." Saul wasn't a prophet, but he came into an environment where the Spirit of prophecy was moving, and it overflowed onto him.

This is what happens in some of our powerful altar calls. In moments of intense worship. In corporate prayer gatherings where the weight of the Spirit rests heavy. Someone might begin to prophesy who doesn't even know they had that gift, but it wasn't their gift being activated, it was the Spirit of prophecy being released in the room.

This is beautiful, but it's also why spiritual maturity and order are essential. Just because someone prophesies once doesn't mean they're called to walk in the *office*. We need discernment in distinguishing the moment from the mantle.

The Gift of Prophecy

This is one of the nine gifts listed in 1 Corinthians 12. It is distinct from the Spirit of prophecy because it operates individually and consistently through a Spirit-filled believer. It doesn't require a certain atmosphere, instead it flows because the Holy Spirit has distributed that gift to that person.

Paul describes the function of this gift clearly in 1 Corinthians 14:3, "But he who prophesies speaks edification and exhortation and comfort to men." This is the gift most common in Spirit-filled churches. Someone begins to speak a word under the unction of the Holy Spirit, and it encourages, builds up, or comforts the Body. It doesn't predict the future. It doesn't correct leadership.

It doesn't bring doctrinal teaching. It speaks life. Strength. Clarity. And it must always align with Scripture.

Prophecy should be tested—not resisted. 1 Thessalonians 5:20–21 says,

"Do not despise prophecies. Test all things;
hold fast what is good."

We don't shut down the gift out of fear of error. We test it, weigh it, and allow spiritual authority to bring order. That's how the gift grows in health and maturity.

It's also important to note: the gift of prophecy does not make someone a prophet. The gift is about function. The office is about calling.

The Office of the Prophet

This is where the weight increases. The office of the prophet is one of the five ministry gifts listed in Ephesians 4:11. Unlike the Spirit of prophecy (which is occasional) or the gift of prophecy (which is functional), the office of the prophet is positional. It's an assignment. A mantle. A divine calling with long-term responsibility and authority in the Body of Christ.

Prophets don't just prophesy, they build. They warn. They guide. They equip. They often function with deeper levels of revelation, dreams, visions, and spiritual discernment. And they don't just speak to individuals—they often speak to leaders, churches, and even regions with messages that carry weight from heaven.

In the New Testament, we see prophets like Agabus who didn't just speak vague encouragement—he gave specific warnings that shaped the direction of churches and apostles. Acts 11:28 says,

> "Then one of them, named Agabus, stood up and showed by the Spirit that there was going to be a great famine..."

Acts 21:10–11 says, "Agabus came down from Judea...and said, 'Thus says the Holy Spirit...'"

Prophets in the New Testament weren't fortune-tellers, they were watchmen. They didn't speak for attention; they spoke with burden. Their words carried consequence. And because of that, the office of the prophet must be tested, affirmed by leadership, and grounded in humility.

Be warned of people who want the title of prophet without the track record of submission, holiness, and spiritual fruit. The office isn't something you claim—it's something confirmed by the Body, proven by maturity, and assigned by God.

Clarifying the Differences

Let's make it plain:

- **The Spirit of Prophecy** is an atmosphere—available to any believer when God's presence is strong.
- **The Gift of Prophecy** is a function—a gift distributed by the Holy Spirit to individuals for the edification of the Body.

- **The Office of the Prophet** is an identity and assignment—a Fivefold Ministry role with governmental responsibility and spiritual authority.

Just because you caught a wave doesn't mean you built the ocean. Just because someone prophesies under the Spirit doesn't mean they're called to walk as a prophet. And that's not a downgrade—it's just a clarification. Every believer can flow in the prophetic. But not every believer is called to walk in the office. We need both—the openness to prophetic flow, and the maturity to discern where we stand.

A Word of Caution and Encouragement

There's a lot of prophetic gifting in the Church today, but there's also a lot of confusion. Clarity brings flow, and submission brings safety. The prophetic is powerful, but it must be handled with reverence and not fear.

If you feel drawn to the prophetic, that's a good thing. Desire it. Pursue it. But stay submitted. Let your leaders guide you. Let the Word anchor you. And don't chase titles—chase truth. The prophetic is God's voice to the Church. And when it flows with order, humility, and clarity—it brings life to everything it touches.

Prophets in the New Testament

When many people hear the word "prophet," their mind goes straight to the Old Testament. You recall Elijah calling down fire from heaven, Isaiah declaring the coming of the Messiah, Jeremiah weeping over the sins of Israel. However, prophecy didn't stop at Malachi and prophets didn't disappear when Jesus ascended.

The New Testament is full of prophetic activity—not just the occasional word of encouragement, but actual prophets, operating in the Church, guiding leaders, confirming direction, and warning of things to come.

The continuation of the prophetic office in the New Testament matters. Why? Because it shows us that prophets weren't just part of an old covenant system—they are part of the structure of the Church Jesus is building today. Let's look at some of the key examples.

Agabus: A Prophet Who Spoke with Precision

Agabus is the clearest example of a New Testament prophet. He's mentioned in two separate places in Acts. Both times, his words carry specific, directional weight. Acts 11:27–28 says:

> "And in these days prophets came from Jerusalem to Antioch. Then one of them, named Agabus, stood up and showed by the Spirit that there was going to be a great famine throughout all the world..."

Notice the details:

- He's explicitly called a prophet.
- He prophesied a specific event (a famine).
- The prophecy was so accurate that the church responded immediately with action—sending relief to the affected regions.

Agabus wasn't vague. He wasn't dramatic. He didn't say "I feel like something hard is coming." He gave names, locations, and details—and it came to pass. That's the mark of a New Testament prophet: clarity, confirmation, and fruit.

Later in Acts 21:10–11, Agabus appears again. This time, he gives a prophetic warning directly to Paul.

> "...a certain prophet named Agabus came down from Judea. When he had come to us, he took Paul's belt, bound his own hands and feet, and said, 'Thus says the Holy Spirit, "So shall the Jews at Jerusalem bind the man who owns this belt...""'"

This is powerful. Agabus doesn't just speak—he demonstrates the word prophetically. He acts it out. This is something we still see in prophetic ministries today: symbolic actions that convey spiritual realities. And once again, his word proves accurate. Paul is arrested, just as Agabus said.

What does this teach us? That prophets in the New Testament didn't just edify, they warned. They prepared the Church. They carried strategic insight. And when received properly, their words shaped the direction of the early Church.

Judas and Silas: Prophets Who Encouraged

Agabus wasn't the only prophet in Acts. In Acts 15:32, we read:

> "Now Judas and Silas, themselves being prophets also, exhorted and strengthened the brethren with many words."

Here we see a different operation. Judas and Silas didn't give directional warnings; they strengthened the Church. They exhorted the believers. This aligns with 1 Corinthians 14:3, where prophecy is meant to edify, exhort, and comfort. This reveals an important truth: not all prophets operate the same way.

Some prophets carry governmental authority—shaping direction, warning leaders, shifting regions. Others function more like prophetic encouragers—strengthening the Church through revelation and words of knowledge. Both are legitimate. Both are needed. But the fruit is the same: the Church is built up, not torn down.

The Prophetic Company in Antioch

One of the clearest glimpses into prophetic structure in the New Testament comes from Acts 13:1–2:

> "Now in the church that was at Antioch there were certain prophets and teachers: Barnabas,

> Simeon who was called Niger, Lucius of Cyrene, Manaen..., and Saul. As they ministered to the Lord and fasted, the Holy Spirit said, 'Now separate to Me Barnabas and Saul for the work to which I have called them.'"

This is a prophetic company—a group of prophets and teachers ministering together in unity. They weren't competing for a microphone. They weren't trying to build a brand. They were seeking the Lord together. And in that atmosphere of worship and fasting, the Spirit gave direction.

The call of Paul and Barnabas—one of the most pivotal missionary assignments in Church history—began in a prophetic environment. This shows us something critical: true prophetic ministry thrives in community not isolation. It doesn't thrive in rebellion, but in community. These prophets were in the Church, submitted to one another, fasting and ministering together. And out of that came divine strategy.

Prophets and the Apostles

In Ephesians 2:20, Paul says the Church is:
> "...built on the foundation of the apostles and prophets, Jesus Christ Himself being the chief cornerstone."

The New Testament doesn't just mention prophets in passing—it places them alongside apostles as foundational leaders.

The apostolic and the prophetic need to work together:

- Apostles lay the foundation.
- Prophets provide revelation.
- Together, they help steer the Church into alignment with heaven.

In a healthy church, you'll often find prophetic voices walking closely with apostolic leadership—not in tension, but in partnership. That's what we see in the early Church. And it's what we're called to walk in today.

Modern Prophets in Apostolic Churches

In East Palo Alto Apostolic Church, my home church, that I have the honor to be the Lead Pastor, prophetic flow is a regular occurrence, but it is never out of order. Prophetic people are raised up, trained, tested, and released, but always under covering.

In our all-night prayer watches, prophetic words have confirmed major decisions. In altar calls, the Spirit has spoken through prophetic insight. But it's not chaos. It's not weird. It's weighty.

New Testament prophecy must come with maturity, character, and submission. Prophets don't just speak, they listen. They don't just declare, they discern.

They don't just say, "God told me", instead they say, "Let's test this together." That's how the early Church handled prophecy and that's how we must walk in it today.

How the Prophetic is Activated

The prophetic isn't something you force. It's something you flow in. And while the gifts of the Spirit are given by grace, the activation of those gifts often requires intentional pursuit. You don't stumble into the prophetic. You grow into it.

In 1 Corinthians 14:1, Paul said, "Pursue love, and desire spiritual gifts, but especially that you may prophesy." The word "desire" in Greek is *zeloo*—it's where we get the word "zeal." It means to burn with passion. Paul is saying: Crave the prophetic. Long for it. Ask for it. Pursue it. Why? Because prophecy builds up the Church. It reveals the mind of God for a moment. It strengthens the weak. It aligns the confused. It gives insight, warning, comfort, and clarity.

If you want to move prophetically, especially with accuracy and authority, it starts in the secret place.

Prayer and Fasting: The Furnace of Revelation

Prophetic flow is birthed in intimacy. In Acts 13, the prophets in Antioch were *"ministering to the Lord and fasting."* That's when the Spirit spoke. That's when direction came. Not while they were working a ministry event. Not while they were posting a prophecy online.

While they were ministering to the Lord. That phrase, "ministering to the Lord", means worship, adoration, sitting at His feet. Creating space to hear. If you want God to speak publicly through you, let Him speak privately to you first.

There have been seasons in my life where I have locked myself in the church building at midnight—no lights, no phone, no distractions. Just me, the Bible, and the presence of God. That's where the prophetic gift in me has been sharpened. Not from a conference, but from a time of consecration.

Fasting quiets the flesh. It tunes out the natural realm so you can tune into the spiritual. When you fast, you are saying, *Lord, Your voice matters more than my appetite. Your direction matters more than my schedule.* That kind of hunger draws heaven's attention.

Ministering to the Lord Before You Minister to People

Too many people want to prophesy over others, but they've stopped ministering to God.

In the tabernacle, the priests ministered to the Lord before they ever turned toward the people. That order still matters today. If you skip the presence, your prophecy becomes performance.

The strongest prophetic voices are those who are anchored in worship. They don't need a platform. They don't chase microphones. They wait on God until their spirit is aligned, and then they speak with precision.

My deepest prophetic moments didn't happen during preaching; they happened in worship. During the quiet in the altar. During a moment when the church was still. That's when the Spirit has whispered. That's when a word of knowledge has flashed across my spirit. That's when the Lord has said, "Call that young man out. I have a word for him."

Prophetic moments are caught, not manufactured. And you only catch them when you've been still enough to recognize His movement.

Spiritual Atmospheres Matter

You can't flow prophetically in an atmosphere that quenches the Spirit. That's why you need to create an atmosphere in your church where the gifts are welcomed—where altar time isn't rushed, where worship is prioritized, where the leaders don't stifle the Spirit in the name of "order."

Now let's be clear: prophecy should never be chaotic. But structure and sensitivity are not enemies. A prophetic church is both submitted to the Word and open to the wind of the Spirit.

The atmosphere you're in affects your ability to discern. That's why prophets must protect their environment. You can't be watching trash on Netflix and expect to hear God clearly. You can't be surrounded by gossip and confusion and expect prophetic accuracy. You have to guard your well.

Prophetic Community Sharpens the Gift

In 1 Samuel 10:10, the Bible says Saul met a group of prophets and as he came into their presence, "the Spirit of God came upon him, and he prophesied among them." Why? Because gifts are contagious. Atmospheres matter. When you surround yourself with prophetic people, the gift in you starts to stir. When you submit to prophetic leadership, your gift sharpens. You start to discern quicker. Speak clearer. Flow freer.

You grow by proximity. You need to be around others who are flowing prophetically. Watch how they carry it. Learn how they discern. Get around those who have gone deeper, not so you can copy them, but so your own spirit can be stirred. Elisha didn't become a prophet by attending a class. He became a prophet by walking with one.

Obedience Is the Trigger

You can pray. You can fast. You can worship and wait, but at some point, you have to speak.

The gifts don't flow through perfection. They flow through obedience. You won't always feel 100% sure. But when the Spirit prompts—say it. Obey quickly. Don't let fear rob you. Don't overthink it. Don't disqualify yourself. Obedience sharpens the gift. Every act of obedience increases your sensitivity. And every moment of hesitation clouds it. The more you obey the whisper, the clearer it gets.

Activation Is God's Invitation

God wants to speak through you. He's looking for a vessel that's hungry enough to seek, humble enough to wait, and bold enough to speak. The prophetic isn't reserved for elite voices. It's for every believer who will make themselves available. So, what are you waiting for? Fast. Pray. Worship. Listen. And when the moment comes—speak.

Prophetic Sensitivity

The prophetic isn't just about speaking. It's about sensing. You can have all the right theology, all the right training, even operate in the gifts of the Spirit—but if you're not sensitive, you'll miss what God is doing in the moment.

Prophetic sensitivity is that inner awareness—that spiritual alertness—that lets you pick up on God's movement in real time. It's what allows you to shift, pause, speak, or stay silent. It's what separates accurate words from noisy ones. It's what keeps the prophetic from becoming performance.

The Bible is full of examples of this kind of awareness. Jesus didn't just preach, He perceived. He didn't just move in power; He moved in response. He said,

"The Son can do nothing of Himself, but what He sees the Father do…" (John 5:19). That's prophetic sensitivity. Seeing what heaven is doing and following its lead.

The Spirit Doesn't Always Move the Same Way

One of the biggest mistakes prophetic people make is trying to repeat what worked last time. The Holy Spirit is not a formula. The Holy Spirit doesn't always flow the same way.

Sometimes God's Spirit is loud. Sometimes it's quiet. Sometimes the Spirit moves during worship. Other times, during the sermon. Sometimes the Spirit interrupts a service before it even begins. And if you're not sensitive, you'll miss it because you were expecting the Spirit to come a certain way.

You have to follow the cloud. In the Old Testament, the cloud represented the presence of God. It moved when God moved. And when it lifted, the people packed up and followed. No questions asked.

Prophetic sensitivity means you stay tuned in—not to the program, not to the plan, but to the presence.

Pay Attention to the Stirring

Many times, the Spirit starts with a stirring, a subtle impression. You're preaching, and suddenly you feel a tug to pause. You're praying, and someone's name drops into your heart. You're worshiping and an urgency rises in your spirit. That's the moment. That's where the prophetic begins.

It's not always a full sentence. Sometimes it's a picture. A word. A flash. A shift in the atmosphere. A moment of stillness where everything in you knows God just entered the room in a new way. When that happens, don't ignore it. Don't push through. Don't silence it in the name of "staying on track." The prophetic doesn't flow in pressure, it flows in sensitivity.

Sensitivity During Preaching

One of the places I tend to operate prophetically is while preaching. Let me explain how this looks.

Sometimes I'll be preaching and suddenly stop, not because I forgot my notes, but because the Spirit whispered. Maybe it's a prophetic word for someone in the room. Maybe it's for a healing or a miracle. Maybe it's a shift in the message. Maybe it's just a moment to pause and let conviction fall. That's what it means to be Spirit-led. Not just to prepare in prayer, but to remain interruptible.

Sometimes, you'll feel like God is asking you to say something that wasn't in your notes. Say it. Sometimes, the whole room will go quiet and the Spirit will fall. Wait. Sometimes, you'll feel the burden lift and you'll know, "That's it." Stop. Prophetic sensitivity gives the Spirit permission to lead.

Discerning Between Emotion and Spirit

Prophetic people must learn to separate their soul from their spirit. Not every emotion is spiritual. Not every tear is prophetic. Not every feeling is a word from God.

Hebrews 4:12 says the Word of God divides between soul and spirit. That means you need the Word—and mature discernment—to know what's truly coming from the Spirit.

If you're not careful, you'll start prophesying your own thoughts. Your own frustrations. Your own assumptions. You'll confuse your burden with God's voice. And that's dangerous.

Sensitivity doesn't mean emotionalism. It means spiritual awareness. It means letting the Spirit lead, not your mood. It means testing the word—not just feeling it. It means slowing down enough to ask, "Is this You, Lord?"

Sensitivity Is Sharpened by Stillness

You can't hear whispers in a noisy room. And you can't discern the Spirit in a noisy life. Prophetic people must learn to live with margins—with space to pray, to listen, to be still. This doesn't mean you need 5 hours of prayer every day. But it does mean you learn to walk slowly enough to catch when the Spirit speaks. It means you put your phone down long enough to hear His voice. It means you don't rush from one task to the next without checking in. It means your life has interruptible moments built in, because God rarely shouts.

Stillness sharpens sensitivity. Stillness quiets the soul so the spirit can rise. Stillness makes room for prophetic clarity.

Prophetic Flow Requires Trust

Sometimes, the Spirit will give you something that doesn't make sense. A word that feels too small. A nudge that seems inconvenient. A phrase that sounds random.

That's where faith comes in. Prophetic flow isn't always about understanding. It's about trusting. It's about saying, "Lord, if this is You—I'll speak. I'll move. I'll obey."

Sometimes God doesn't give the whole sentence until you say the first word. That's prophetic sensitivity. Saying "yes" before you have it all. Moving with the cloud. Trusting the whisper.

The More You Listen, the Sharper You Get

You want to grow in the prophetic? Start paying attention. To the stillness. To the stirring. To the subtle shifts in your spirit. Learn what it feels like when God is near. Learn how the atmosphere changes. Learn what happens in your body, your spirit, your thoughts—when the Spirit begins to move.

And then, when you sense it, respond. That's how prophetic sensitivity grows. Through practice, proximity, obedience, and stillness. Because the prophetic doesn't just come through boldness. It comes through awareness.

CHAPTER 4

The Gifts of Revelation

The Gifts of the Spirit

Before we dive into the first gift, let's set the stage. Paul introduces the gifts of the Spirit in 1 Corinthians 12:1, saying:

"Now concerning spiritual gifts, brethren, I do not want you to be ignorant."

This tells us two things right away: (1) These gifts are *spiritual*—they're supernatural, not natural. (2) Ignorance is a danger—the Church is prone to either fear them, fake them, or forget them.

That's why this section exists. To break the ignorance. To teach, clarify, and activate. Because these gifts are *still for today*, and they weren't given for status—they were given for service.

The nine gifts of the Spirit are commonly grouped into three categories:

- **Revelation Gifts** (Knowing):
  Word of Wisdom
  Word of Knowledge
  Discerning of Spirits

- **Power Gifts** (Doing):
  Faith
  Gifts of Healing
  Working of Miracles

- **Vocal Gifts** (Speaking):
  Prophecy
  Diverse Kinds of Tongues
  Interpretation of Tongues

We'll start with the Revelation Gifts—these gifts help you *know* what you couldn't know on your own. They come by the Spirit and give divine insight, often in moments of decision, crisis, or ministry.

Let's begin with the Word of Wisdom.

Word of Wisdom: Supernatural Guidance for Future Situations

The Word of Wisdom is not "a wise word." It's not clever advice. It's not experience. It's not intelligence.

The Word of Wisdom is a supernatural revelation of what to do in a situation—particularly something relating to the *future*. It's a piece of God's wisdom dropped into your spirit for a specific moment or decision. It's not the full mind of God—it's a *word*. A fragment. A portion. Just enough to guide the next step, but it carries divine strategy.

Biblical Example: Jesus and the Net

In Luke 5, Jesus tells Peter to cast his net on the other side of the boat. Peter is a professional fisherman, he knows this lake, he's been out all night, and he's caught nothing.

> "Master, we have toiled all night and caught nothing; nevertheless at Your word I will let down the net." (Luke 5:5)

What happens? A net-breaking, boat-sinking catch. That wasn't fishing knowledge. That wasn't luck. That was a Word of Wisdom. Jesus gave a divinely timed instruction, and when Peter obeyed, the supernatural was released.

That's how the Word of Wisdom works. It gives insight for something *ahead of you*, and when you obey, the door opens.

When It Manifests

The Word of Wisdom often shows up in prayer, when seeking direction. It shows up in counseling, when helping someone navigate a tough decision. It shows up during ministry, when needing to know the next step. It shows up in crisis, when the natural options seem impossible. Sometimes, it will come as a phrase. Sometimes a mental picture. Sometimes an idea that suddenly carries clarity and peace. It may not always make sense at first, but it will always bear fruit when obeyed.

Start With the Soil

When I was the Supervisor of the Region of South America, living in Chile, I was praying about whether to launch a new ministry in the country of Peru. There were financial concerns, leadership uncertainties, and spiritual opposition. But in prayer, the Lord gave me a simple phrase: "Start with the soil."

I didn't understand at first, but as I kept praying, I felt led to visit that country and walk the grounds. As I did, I began interceding over the territory. A few weeks later, doors opened miraculously. Finances came through. Local leaders stepped up. And what began as confusion became clarity. The Word of Wisdom didn't come with a 10-step plan. It came with *one phrase*. And when I obeyed it, everything else followed.

Characteristics of the Word of Wisdom

The Word of Wisdom is a supernatural insight that doesn't come from intellect or experience—it comes directly from the Spirit of God. It's not a brainstorm, a good idea, or a clever solution. It's divine intelligence. And when it comes, it often carries qualities that make it stand out from natural reasoning.

One of the first things you'll notice is that it's clearer than your own thoughts. When the Word of Wisdom is released, it cuts through mental clutter. What felt tangled or overwhelming just moments ago becomes simple and focused. It has a way of making complex problems seem solvable—not by explaining every detail, but by shining a light on the next right step.

Another mark of the Word of Wisdom is its timeliness. It doesn't always come early, but it's never late. Often, it shows up in the middle of a dilemma—when a door is closing, when a crisis is unfolding, or when the path ahead looks foggy. It might not give you a five-year plan, but it gives you what you need *right now*.

Words of Wisdom also carry a weight of peace. This can't be overstated. When the Word of Wisdom is truly from God, it won't stir panic or anxiety—it will quiet the storm in your mind. It might stretch you. It might call you into the unknown. But it will carry the peace that passes understanding. That peace is the signature of the Holy Spirit.

The Word of Wisdom is often uncommon—meaning it doesn't always align with what seems logical. It might lead you in a direction that contradicts your instincts, your training, or even the advice of well-meaning friends. But it won't contradict the Word of God. That's why spiritual discernment is so important. God's ways are higher, and the Word of Wisdom will often reflect that.

Sometimes the Word of Wisdom feels like a whisper, a subtle impression, not a booming command. Other times, it can come through someone else's mouth without them realizing it. A sermon. A prayer. A phrase in conversation. Suddenly, something clicks. Your spirit leaps. That's when you know: *God just spoke.*

It's also important to remember: the Word of Wisdom doesn't always come with an explanation. God might give you the "what" before He gives you the "why." You may feel led to pray for someone, cancel a trip, sow a financial seed, or take a leap of faith—and not understand the reason until later. But when it's truly a Word of Wisdom, obedience will always lead to fruit.

In short, the Word of Wisdom is:

- Clearer than your thoughts
- Timely and precise
- Marked by supernatural peace
- Often uncommon or unexpected
- Spiritually weighty, yet simple
- Rooted in Scripture and alignment with God's character

Once you learn to recognize these qualities, you'll become more confident in distinguishing God's wisdom from your own reasoning. As you grow in sensitivity and obedience, the Word of Wisdom will flow more freely, not just for you, but through you.

Responding to the Word of Wisdom

When the Word of Wisdom comes, it often arrives in a moment of stillness—a phrase that drops into your spirit, an idea that interrupts your natural train of thought, or a sense of clarity that seems to come out of nowhere. It's easy to brush it off. It's easy to second-guess and move on. But that's where many miss it. The Word of Wisdom must be *handled with care*, not with fear, but with intention. It's a gift, and like any gift from God, it's meant to be stewarded.

The first thing you should do is write it down. Don't assume you'll remember it later. What seems vivid in the moment can fade with time. Writing it down gives space for reflection, clarity, and confirmation. Sometimes, what doesn't make sense now will become clear in hindsight, but only if you captured it in the moment.

Once you've written it down, take it back into prayer. Ask the Lord, "What are You saying through this? What do You want me to do with it?" You don't have to force interpretation, just stay open. Sometimes the Lord will confirm it immediately. Other times, it unfolds over time, like layers peeling back until the full picture comes into view.

Always weigh it against the Word of God. The Holy Spirit never contradicts Scripture. A true Word of Wisdom will always align with God's character and truth. It won't feed your ego, validate sin, or lead you away from godly counsel. It may stretch you—but it won't contradict what's already been written.

For major decisions, don't isolate. Bring it to spiritual leadership or trusted mentors. Submitting a word to spiritual covering is not a sign of weakness—it's a mark of maturity. God places spiritual authority in your life to protect you, not control you. If the word is from God, it will stand up to accountability.

Finally, and this is where many get stuck, you have to obey. Revelation without obedience is useless. The blessing is not in knowing what to do—it's in *doing it*. Sometimes the Word of Wisdom won't make sense until after you step out. Obedience unlocks the next step.

So, if God gives you a Word, don't delay. Don't wait for it to be comfortable. Don't wait for ten confirmations. Write it down. Pray it through. Test it by the Word. Submit it to covering. And when peace settles in your spirit, move. The Word of Wisdom isn't just insight—it's an *invitation*.

From Revelation to Action

The Word of Wisdom is powerful—but only if you act on it. Too many people receive divine insight and then hesitate. They wait for more information. More signs. More clarity. But sometimes, the clarity comes in the doing. Obedience activates what the Word was meant to unlock.

Don't treat revelation as entertainment. It's not for collecting—it's for *moving*. When God speaks, don't delay. When God instructs, don't debate. When God gives you a Word—*go with it*. Because one Word from God is better than a thousand opinions.

Word of Knowledge: Supernatural Insight into the Present or the Past

If the Word of Wisdom is heaven's instruction for the future, the Word of Knowledge is heaven's revelation of the present or past. It's when the Holy Spirit gives you information that you couldn't possibly know on your own—a divine download that brings clarity, conviction, and confirmation.

This gift often works like a spotlight. It shines on something hidden, something beneath the surface, and exposes it—not to embarrass, but to bring healing, deliverance, or direction. It might be a name, a physical condition, a location, a past event, or a secret pain. And when spoken in obedience, it opens hearts like nothing else can.

Jesus and the Woman at the Well

One of the clearest examples in Scripture is found in John 4. Jesus is speaking with the Samaritan woman at the well. At first, the conversation seems ordinary—water, worship, and the mountain debate. But then Jesus shifts gears and says, "Go, call your husband." She responds, "I have no husband." And then He delivers the Word of Knowledge:

> "You have well said, 'I have no husband,' for you have had five husbands, and the one whom you now have is not your husband."
> (John 4:17–18)

That's the Word of Knowledge in action. Jesus revealed something about her past that He had no natural way of knowing. And what happened next? She left her water pot, ran into the city, and said, "Come, see a Man who told me all things that I ever did. Could this be the Christ?" (John 4:29). The Word of Knowledge broke through her skepticism. It turned a casual conversation into a divine encounter that led to a city-wide awakening.

How the Word of Knowledge Operates

This gift doesn't always arrive the same way. Sometimes it comes as a mental impression—a thought that enters your mind during prayer or while ministering. You might suddenly think of a name, a date, or a condition. Other times, it's a physical sensation—you may feel pain in a certain part of your body that doesn't belong to you, but is tied to someone else's need. It can also come as a picture, vision, or word that lingers in your spirit and won't let go.

However it comes, the key is to stay yielded and not overanalyze. You don't have to be 100% sure before stepping out. Faith is part of the flow. The more you obey those subtle nudges, the more clearly the gift begins to operate.

What's It For

The Word of Knowledge is never for gossip or control, it's for breakthrough. When someone realizes that God knows exactly what they're going through, walls come down. Hardened hearts melt. Tears flow. Faith rises. It reminds people that God sees them and that alone is often enough to open the door to healing or repentance.

In my ministry, the Word of Knowledge has operated many times during altar calls or street evangelism. There have been moments when the Lord revealed someone's childhood trauma, or called out a name connected to hidden abuse—and the result wasn't shame, it was freedom. Because the Word of Knowledge doesn't expose to condemn, it reveals to redeem.

Staying Grounded

As with all the gifts, the Word of Knowledge must be tested and submitted. It should never contradict Scripture. It should never be used to manipulate. And it should never be treated like a show. The gift may draw attention, but the goal is transformation. If the fruit isn't healing, conviction, or breakthrough—it might be another voice you're hearing.

This is why it's vital to stay in the Word, stay in prayer, and stay under spiritual authority. The purer the vessel, the clearer the word. And the clearer the word, the greater the impact.

Discerning of Spirits

The gift of discerning of spirits is one of the most misunderstood—and most needed—gifts in the Body of Christ. This gift is not about suspicion. This gift is not having a gut instinct. And this gift is not natural intuition. This is a supernatural ability given by the Holy Spirit to recognize what kind of spirit is at work—whether it's the Spirit of God, a demonic spirit, or even just a human spirit.

The gift of discerning of spirits pulls back the curtain. It reveals what's operating beneath the surface—beyond what the eye can see or the ear can hear. While some gifts reveal information (like the word of knowledge), this gift reveals influence. It helps you understand *why* something is happening and *what* spirit is behind it.

1 Corinthians 12:10 lists it clearly: "...to another discerning of spirits..." It doesn't say "the gift of discernment." That's a common misquote. This isn't about having a generally wise or perceptive nature. This is *discerning of spirits*, plural. That includes the Holy Spirit, angelic spirits, demonic spirits, and the human spirit.

Why This Gift Matters

We are in a spiritual war. The battle isn't just about decisions, habits, or emotions, it's about spirits. Behind confusion is a spirit. Behind fear is a spirit. Behind deception is a spirit. And if we don't discern it, we'll waste time fighting in the flesh what can only be addressed in the Spirit.

This gift protects the Church. It exposes counterfeit anointings. It calls out impure motives wrapped in spiritual language. And it also encourages—because it recognizes the move of the Holy Spirit and confirms when God is truly at work. Without this gift, churches tolerate things they should cast out and cast out things they should embrace.

How This Gift Operates

Discerning of spirits doesn't always come as a dramatic vision or a booming voice. Often, it begins as a sense, a sudden awareness, a deep knowing, a check in your spirit that something isn't right.

Sometimes, your body reacts before your mind catches up—you feel nauseous in certain places, heavy in your chest when someone speaks, or disturbed in prayer without understanding why.

Other times, this gift reveals purity. You walk into a room and feel peace, not from the environment, but from the Spirit. You meet someone and immediately sense they carry God's presence. You hear someone minister and you recognize the flow of the Holy Spirit before they finish a sentence.

Earlier in this book, I shared an experience of stepping off a plane and sensing a dark presence. I heard in my spirit, "We know you're here." That encounter was one of the clearest examples in my life of the gift of discerning of spirits in operation. Right away I knew that the principality over that region had taken notice, not of me, but of the authority I carried in the Spirit. That moment wasn't about fear. It was about awareness. When you walk in spiritual authority, the enemy doesn't wait until you grab a microphone to react. He senses it the moment you arrive.

The gift of discerning of spirits sharpens your awareness, not just of the demonic, but of divine assignments. Sometimes the Holy Spirit will highlight someone to you in a service—not because they look troubled, but because their spirit is crying out. And when you walk in this gift, you begin to pick up on those cries.

What This Gift Is Not

Discerning of spirits is not the same as being critical. It's not an excuse to be suspicious, paranoid, or controlling. True discernment flows with the fruit of the Spirit—love, joy, peace, patience, gentleness. It doesn't bring confusion, it brings clarity.

Some people say, "I'm just discerning," but really, they don't trust anybody. That's not discernment, that's a wound. And if you're not healed, your perception will always be twisted. Wounded discernment often looks like hypervigilance, spiritual superiority, or a need to control everything around you. But that's not the Spirit—that's trauma wearing a prophetic mask.

The goal of discernment isn't to tear people down—it's to build the Church up. It's meant to guard, not gossip. To protect, not punish. To align, not divide. When this gift is used properly, it brings peace and order. But when it's unchecked, it breeds suspicion and strife. That's why even discernment must be submitted to spiritual authority. Because no matter how gifted you are, if your heart is off—your discernment will be too.

Before moving forward, take a moment to ask: Is my discernment coming from the Spirit or from a past hurt I haven't surrendered yet? Have I been calling suspicion "discernment"? Are there wounds, betrayals, or disappointments that might be clouding my spiritual perception? Have I submitted my discernment to godly authority—or have I been operating on my own?

Let the Lord bring anything to the surface that needs healing. Write it down. Bring it into prayer. Healing is part of the flow.

Growing in Discernment

Just like with any spiritual gift, the more you use it, the sharper it becomes. And the more you submit it, the safer it becomes.

Want to grow in discernment? Just like any other gift, you must be consistent in the following:

- Stay in the Word. The Bible is the filter for all revelation.
- Stay in prayer. The more time you spend with the Holy Spirit, the more you recognize God's movement.
- Stay submitted. Covering keeps your discernment accountable.
- Stay humble. If you think you always know what spirit is at work, you've probably already missed it.

God is raising up a discerning Church—not just prophetic, but discerning. A Church that doesn't fall for charisma over character. A Church that sees past the surface. A Church that recognizes when the Holy Spirit is moving and when something else is trying to infiltrate.

In the days ahead, this gift will be vital. Because the enemy doesn't always show up with horns and red lights. Sometimes he shows up with a mic and a platform. So, ask God to sharpen your discernment—not to criticize, but to protect, to align, and to flow with purity in the Spirit.

Deliverance: A Forgotten Expression of Discernment

One of the most overlooked applications of the gift of discerning of spirits is deliverance—the casting out of unclean spirits. While deliverance is not a listed gift in 1

Corinthians 12, it is often the natural result when this gift is in operation.

Discernment reveals what's hiding. It unmasks the invisible. And sometimes, what is revealed must be confronted, not with counseling, but with spiritual authority.

Jesus didn't just preach, teach, and heal, He delivered. In fact, His earliest miracles included casting out demons. He didn't send them to therapy; He cast them out with a word. Mark 16:17 says, "And these signs will follow those who believe: In My name they will cast out demons…"

Remember that power doesn't cast out demons, authority does. Deliverance is not about volume or hype. It's not about emotion. It's about spiritual jurisdiction. That jurisdiction comes through submission to God's Word and God's order.

When someone is bound, and the Spirit highlights it to you—it's not just so you can see it. It's so you can do something about it. That's where the other gifts often come into play: a word of knowledge may reveal the root, the gift of faith may rise in the moment, and miracles may be released as the spirit is cast out. Discernment opens the door, but authority walks through it. You don't counsel out a demon. You cast it out.

In deliverance, discretion is key. You don't expose people to shame them—you cover them so they can be restored. True deliverance doesn't cause confusion. It brings clarity. It brings peace. It leaves a person "clothed and in their right mind" (Mark 5:15).

In the days ahead, as the Church steps deeper into spiritual operation, we must recover deliverance. Not as a strange side-ministry, but as a normal part of the Spirit-filled life. And it starts with discerning the spirit behind the problem—and having the authority to deal with it.

CHAPTER 5

The Gifts of Power

"The Kingdom of God is not in word, but in power." 1 Corinthians 4:20

The Gifts of Power are the supernatural expressions of God's might working through human vessels. We've looked at the Revelation Gifts, which are about knowing something beyond your intellect. Now let's examine the Gifts of Power, which are doing something that only God can do.

The Gifts of Power are the gifts that shake atmospheres. They break chains. They part seas, shut the mouths of lions, and raise the dead. The Gifts of Power don't operate through hype or emotion—they operate through faith, obedience, and surrender.

The Gifts of Power are all over the Book of Acts. But too often, the modern Church has tried to explain away the supernatural because we're afraid of what we can't control. Do not try to sanitize the Book of Acts. Jesus didn't just preach the Kingdom—He demonstrated it. And if we're going to be His Body in the earth today, we have to do the same. In this section, we'll look at the three Gifts of Power:

- The Gift of Faith
- The Gifts of Healings
- The Working of Miracles

These gifts are not for spiritual elites. They're for anyone who is willing to step out of comfort and into the current of God's power. They are just as necessary now as they were in the first century.

Let's begin with the Gift of Faith—the doorway to the miraculous.

Gift of Faith

Faith is the currency of the Kingdom. There is a faith that goes beyond belief—beyond reason—beyond even hope. It's called the Gift of Faith. This gift isn't just about trusting God in general, it's a sudden, supernatural download of confidence that God is going to act, and nothing can shake you from it.

What Is the Gift of Faith?

The Gift of Faith is not the same as saving faith (Romans 10:9) or the fruit of faithfulness (Galatians 5:22). Every believer has saving faith, and all should grow in consistent, daily faith. But the Gift of Faith is a supernatural surge, a divine impartation that empowers you to believe for something radical in the moment. It's the ability to stand still in the middle of chaos and declare, *God is going to move—I don't know how, but I know He will.* It's what Daniel had in the lions' den. It's what Abraham had on the mountain with Isaac. It's what Peter had when he stepped out of the boat to walk on water.

It's not mustered up. It's not manufactured. It comes upon you by the Spirit, and when it does, fear vanishes and boldness rises.

How It Operates

The Gift of Faith often shows up in moments of crisis or need. You may not even realize what's happening until afterward. You just know something rose up inside you, and you couldn't doubt it if you tried.

The Gift of Faith might manifest in declaring healing over someone without hesitation, stepping into a hostile environment with unshakable peace, giving a bold prophetic word with no fear of man, or acting on an instruction from God that makes no logical sense

Biblical Example: Elijah and the Drought

In 1 Kings 17, Elijah walks into the king's court and declares: "There shall not be dew nor rain these years, except at my word." That's bold. That's supernatural confidence. That's the Gift of Faith.

Elijah wasn't guessing. He wasn't hoping. He knew. Why? Because the Spirit of the Lord had spoken—and when the Gift of Faith hits, hesitation leaves.

Biblical Example: Jesus Cursing the Fig Tree

(Mark 11:12–14) Jesus sees a fig tree with no fruit, and He says, "Let no one eat fruit from you ever again." The next day, the disciples are shocked to see it withered from the roots.

What happened? Jesus operated in the Gift of Faith—and things shifted instantly in the spiritual realm, even though it took a moment for the natural to catch up.

Personal Example:

There was a time when I was ministering in a service and the Spirit of the Lord prompted in my spirit to say, "There is someone here who has a disease in their blood. The doctors said it's incurable, but the Lord is healing you now." That wasn't a guess. That wasn't a general encouragement. It was a moment of divine knowing—a flash of the supernatural—and I knew without a doubt that God had just healed them.

After the service, a woman came forward weeping. The doctors had diagnosed her with a rare blood condition. She had kept it secret, but in that moment, God confirmed His word—and the healing began. That's what the Gift of Faith does. It pierces the fog. It creates an atmosphere for miracles.

Responding to the Gift of Faith

If you feel that supernatural surge, don't resist it. Speak it. Step into it. God doesn't give the Gift of Faith for decoration—He gives it to activate something in the atmosphere.

Sometimes, the gift is the only thing standing between a breakthrough and a breakdown. Your obedience might be the trigger that releases heaven's power. So don't shrink back. Don't overthink it. If God puts it in your spirit—say it, do it, believe it.

Gifts of Healings

God Still Heals, and He Wants to Use You.

There is no clearer demonstration of the compassion and power of Jesus than healing. When Jesus walked the earth, healing wasn't a side ministry, it was a central part of His mission. He healed the blind, raised the dead, cleansed lepers, and made the paralyzed walk. And the good news is: He hasn't changed. Hebrews 13:8 says: "Jesus Christ is the same yesterday, today, and forever." If He healed then, He heals now. One of the primary ways He releases that healing is through the Gifts of Healings.

Why It's Plural: "Gifts of Healings"

"To another faith by the same Spirit, to another gifts of healings by the same Spirit," (1 Corinthians 12:9). This is the only spiritual gift listed in 1 Corinthians 12 that's double plural—"gifts" (plural) of "healings" (plural). Why? Because this gift isn't one-size-fits-all.

Some people carry a particular anointing for emotional healing: ministering to trauma, grief, and mental wounds. Others carry an anointing for spiritual healing such as restoring a backslider back to God. Others have seen God use them more in physical healing—cancer, pain, mobility issues. Some flow in healing for specific types of conditions: deafness, infertility, chronic disease. Some are used more when laying hands on individuals, while others release healing over a crowd or region. Healing flows in different ways through different vessels, but all of it comes from the same Spirit.

What the Gift Does

The Gifts of Healings are supernatural empowerments to restore health to the body, soul, or spirit. It's not limited to what doctors can explain. It's not subject to prognosis. It's the power of the cross breaking into the present moment.

Sometimes healing comes through a touch. Other times through a word. Sometimes it's triggered by obedience, like dipping in water or stepping forward. And often, healing requires faith on the part of both the minister and the recipient.

Why Healing Still Matters

There's a false belief in some circles that healing was only for the early church—that it ceased with the Apostles. Scripture, however, never teaches that. The book of Acts shows us what *normal* Christianity should look like—not the exception. James 5:14–15 says:

> "Is anyone among you sick? Let him call for the elders of the church… and the prayer of faith will save the sick, and the Lord will raise him up."

That wasn't written to the Apostles, it was written to the Church. That includes us.

Jesus didn't just come to save your soul—He came to heal your whole being. Isaiah 53:5 says, "By His stripes, we are healed." Healing is in the atonement. It's part of the covenant. And God still confirms His word with signs following.

Obedience-Led Healing

One Sunday, while ministering in a service, I was prompted by the Holy Spirit to call for a woman who had been dealing with severe pain in her hip. I didn't know who it was, but the impression was clear. So, I spoke it out: "There's a woman here with pain in your right hip—the Lord is healing you right now." A woman hesitated, then raised her hand. "That's me," she said through tears. I walked over and was about to lay hands on her when the Spirit said, *"Tell her to lift her hands and begin to thank Me before you touch her."* So, I obeyed. She lifted her hands. And the moment she said, "Thank You, Jesus," her body jolted—the pain was gone. Instantly.

It wasn't about theatrics. It wasn't hype. It was obedience. The healing wasn't in the hand—it was in the instruction. That's often how the Gifts of Healings work: God gives a specific instruction, and when we respond in faith, the power is released.

Pray for the Sick

I'll never forget this: A young girl was brought to the altar by her parents, and they said she had been having seizures. They were desperate. They had been to doctors. They were scared. As I laid hands on her, I felt a tangible peace settle in the atmosphere. I prayed a simple prayer—no yelling, no theatrics—just a declaration of healing in Jesus' name. Weeks later, the family came back with tears in their eyes. They said, "Since that night, she hasn't had a single seizure."

How to Walk in This Gift

The Gifts of Healings don't require you to be a medical expert. You don't need a degree. What you need is compassion, sensitivity to the Spirit, and bold obedience. Here's how to prepare your spirit:

- Spend time in prayer, asking God to use you as a vessel of healing.
- Read the healing miracles of Jesus and let faith rise.
- Ask for the gift—1 Corinthians 14:1 says to "earnestly desire spiritual gifts."
- When you sense the prompting, step out. Don't wait for a choir or a feeling. Just obey.

Sometimes God will tell you to lay hands. Sometimes He'll say, "Have them walk across the room." Sometimes He'll whisper, "Tell them they're already healed." Don't overcomplicate it. Just follow the nudge—the healing is in the flow.

Final Thought

Healing is not about proving something—it's about revealing Someone. When people are healed, Jesus is glorified. The kingdom is advanced. Faith is stirred and lives are changed.

So don't let fear stop you. Don't let a past disappointment silence you. Keep praying. Keep obeying. Because healing still flows—and God wants it to flow through you.

While we boldly declare that God still heals today, we also recognize that not every prayer results in an immediate or visible miracle. This doesn't mean the gift is absent or that faith is lacking. Faith trusts that God is sovereign and that His ways are higher than ours, even when we don't understand the outcome.

The Apostle Paul, despite his powerful ministry, wrote that he left Trophimus sick in Miletus (2 Timothy 4:20). This shows us that the operation of the gifts of healings must remain rooted in obedience, not results. Sometimes healing is instant, sometimes progressive. But always—it is God who heals. Our role is to trust, to pray, and to obey. The outcome is in His hands.

Working of Miracles

The working of miracles is one of the most awe-inspiring gifts in the believer's arsenal. It goes beyond healing, beyond wisdom—this is when God suspends the laws of nature and manifests His power in a way that defies explanation.

This isn't just about praying and hoping. It's about stepping out in faith and working the miracle. The very language Paul uses in 1 Corinthians 12, "the working of miracles"—implies action, motion, participation. This gift often requires obedience to a Spirit-led instruction that may feel unusual, but it's in that obedience that the supernatural is released.

---

*Miracles don't just happen when we believe—
they often happen when we act.*

I've seen that miracles are usually connected to obedience. You don't wait for the miracle to manifest—you walk into it by doing what God shows you to do.

Miracles Through Action

I prayed for this gift for twenty years. One morning while I was praying, the Holy Spirit prompted me by saying, "Work the miracle." That instruction wasn't vague; it was a charge to act in faith.

While ministering in a church service, I called to pray for a woman who had been bound to a wheelchair for many years. I didn't wait for the woman to be healed before moving. I moved, and the miracle followed. Like Jesus telling the man with the withered hand to stretch it out—the miracle was in the stretching.

Sometimes the working of miracles involves doing something in the natural as an act of faith: snapping fingers near a deaf ear, lifting a limb, walking someone forward, or instructing someone to act in a way they couldn't before. These physical actions aren't magical; they're acts of obedience that unlock God's power.

I remember being in a service where I felt a surge of boldness come over me. The Lord impressed on me, "Don't wait—work the miracle." I walked up to a man who was suffering physically and felt the Spirit tell me to take a bold step and I obeyed. The moment I acted, the power of God hit him, and healing flowed.

This mirrors the example of Jesus when He healed the blind man by spitting on the ground, making mud, and placing it on the man's eyes (John 9:6–7). The man wasn't healed until he went and washed. The miracle was released through obedience.

Biblical Foundation

Scripture is full of examples of this type of miracle-working faith:

- Jesus turning water into wine (John 2): He told the servants to fill the jars with water—and it became wine after their obedience.
- Elijah calling down fire from heaven (1 Kings 18): He rebuilt the altar, soaked it in water, and God responded to his action with fire.
- Paul and Silas worshipping in prison (Acts 16): They didn't wait for deliverance before praising, they praised, and then the chains broke.

Miracles are not just about power—they are about alignment. When you align with heaven's instruction, heaven responds with power.

The Role of Boldness

This gift definitely requires boldness. You cannot work miracles timidly. The early Church walked in this kind of boldness, not arrogance, but Holy Ghost confidence. Acts 4:29–30 records their prayer:

> "Now, Lord, look on their threats, and grant to Your servants that with all boldness they may speak Your word, by stretching out Your hand to heal, and that signs and wonders may be done through the name of Your holy Servant Jesus."

They didn't ask God to make miracles happen in private. They asked for boldness to act in public.

When you step out, God steps in. But if you wait for a safe moment, you'll miss it. Miracles often come when you obey a risky prompting.

CHAPTER 6

The Vocal Gifts

If the gifts of revelation are about seeing, and the gifts of power are about doing—then the vocal gifts are about speaking. These are the gifts that release the sound of heaven through human vessels.

In the beginning, God spoke—and creation responded. He didn't build the world with His hands. He released it with His voice. From Genesis to Revelation, we see one consistent truth: God moves through words.

The vocal gifts—prophecy, diverse kinds of tongues, and interpretation of tongues—are how God speaks through His Church today. They are supernatural utterances. Spirit-breathed words that don't originate in human thought, but flow from a surrendered heart. This is why the enemy fights these gifts so hard. Because when the Church finds its voice—hell loses ground.

Some people are afraid of these gifts. Maybe they've seen them abused. Maybe they've heard strange things or been in services where things got out of order. But we don't throw out the gifts because of misuse. We go back to the Word. We ask the Holy Spirit to teach us. We anchor ourselves in truth—and we press in.

Paul didn't say to avoid these gifts. He said in 1 Thessalonians 5:19–21:

> "Do not quench the Spirit. Do not despise prophecies. Test all things; hold fast what is good."

The vocal gifts are powerful. When they're flowing under the direction of the Holy Spirit, they bring freedom, clarity, and breakthrough. They remind the Church that this isn't just a religion—it's a relationship with a God who still speaks.

So don't be afraid of the sound of heaven. Don't silence the voice of the Spirit. Instead, ask God to use your mouth for His glory. Because when God speaks, things shift.

The Gift of Prophecy

If there's one gift that stirs people's curiosity, and also causes confusion, it's prophecy. Some think it's fortune-telling. Some think it died with the apostles. Some treat it like a spiritual slot machine, hoping to "pull a word" out of the air. But prophecy is far more sacred than that. It's not a gimmick. It's not hype. It's the voice of God flowing through a yielded vessel to bring strength, encouragement, and alignment to His people.

Paul put it like this in 1 Corinthians 14:3:

"But he who prophesies speaks edification
and exhortation and comfort to men."

That's the heartbeat of prophecy: to edify (build up), exhort (stir up), and comfort (lift up).

What the Gift of Prophecy Is

Prophecy is a supernatural utterance in a known language. It's when the Spirit of God gives you words to speak, not from your own understanding, but straight from the heart of God. You might sense a phrase, a sentence, or even an entire message that flows through you in prayer, worship, or during a service. You're not guessing. You're not making it up. You're tuning in to heaven's signal—and releasing what you hear.

This is not the office of a prophet. That's different. The gift of prophecy is available to any Spirit-filled believer who is willing to listen, discern, and obey. Paul said in 1 Corinthians 14:1:

"Pursue love, and desire spiritual gifts, but
especially that you may prophesy."

Why *especially* prophecy? Because prophecy strengthens the Church. It realigns people with God's voice. It awakens hearts. It reminds the Body that God is present, personal, and speaking.

What Prophecy Sounds Like

Prophecy doesn't always come in thunder. Sometimes it's a whisper. It can sound like a word of encouragement during altar ministry. It can come through a prayer that suddenly shifts from "you" talking to God, to Him talking through you. It can feel like an urgency in your spirit that you can't shake—a word burning on the inside until it's released.

And often, it won't make full sense to you. That's a good thing. It keeps you humble. When you prophesy by the Spirit, it's not your intellect—it's His inspiration. Your job is obedience.

I've seen this over and over—moments where the Lord drops a simple phrase into my spirit, and I speak it over someone at the altar. They begin to weep. Why? Because it's exactly what they've been praying about. I didn't know it, but the Holy Ghost did. That's the power of prophecy. It bypasses the surface and speaks straight to the heart.

Guardrails for the Gift

Because prophecy is powerful, it must also be handled carefully. There are some key principles to keep in mind:

1. **It must align with Scripture.** God will never contradict His Word. If a prophecy goes against the Bible—toss it. Period.
2. **It must flow from love.** Prophecy is not a weapon to control people. It's a gift to edify them. If your heart is not rooted in love, don't speak.
3. **It must be judged.** Paul said in 1 Corinthians 14:29: "Let two or three prophets speak and let the others judge." No prophetic word is above testing. Mature leaders should weigh what's spoken. The Holy Spirit is not afraid of accountability.
4. **It must be delivered in humility.** Prophecy should open hearts, not shut them down.
5. **It must point to Jesus.** Revelation 19:10 says, "The testimony of Jesus is the spirit of prophecy." True prophecy glorifies Christ, not the person speaking.

Prophecy in the Local Church

Every church that desires the supernatural must make room for prophecy, but also teach people how to move in it biblically. You don't need a microphone to prophesy. You can release a word during prayer time, at the altar, or even in conversation. You can prophesy through a text, a song, or a whisper in someone's ear at just the right moment. The setting may vary, but the Spirit is the same.

And yes, it should be done decently and in order. Paul devoted an entire chapter (1 Corinthians 14) to helping churches steward this gift properly. Why? Because when prophecy is healthy, the church becomes alive. People realize, "God knows me. He sees me. He's with me."

Final Thoughts

You don't have to be loud to prophesy. You don't have to be weird. You just have to yield. Start with the Word. Start in prayer. And when you sense the Lord stirring something in your spirit—speak it in love, speak it humbly, and watch how the Holy Spirit moves through it.

The gift of prophecy is not just for platforms—it's for everyday moments. It's for building people up. For breaking spiritual heaviness. For realigning the Church with the heart of God.

So don't just admire the gift. Desire it. Pursue it. Practice it. God is still speaking. He's just looking for someone who will say *yes*.

Gift of Diverse Kinds of Tongues: Heaven's Language for Earth's Edification

Speaking in tongues is one of the most unique and misunderstood manifestations of the Holy Spirit. It can be controversial, but only when it's not understood in its biblical context. The enemy has worked overtime to distort and discredit this gift because he knows how powerful it really is.

The gift of diverse kinds of tongues—also called "varieties of tongues"—is not just emotional expression. It is a supernatural language, given by the Holy Spirit, that bypasses the mind and releases direct communication with God. 1 Corinthians 12:10 names it clearly:

> "...to another divers kinds of tongues; to another the interpretation of tongues" (King James Version).

This chapter isn't about tongues as Spirit baptism—although that's a foundational moment in every Spirit-filled believer's life. This chapter is about the spiritual gift of tongues in a corporate setting, meant for the edification of the Church when coupled with interpretation.

The Difference Between Prayer Tongues and the Gift of Tongues

Let's clear up a common confusion: There is a difference between praying in tongues and the gift of tongues for public ministry.

Praying in tongues is your personal prayer language. It builds you up spiritually (Jude 1:20). It's a form of communion with God. Paul said, "I thank my God I speak with tongues more than you all" (1 Corinthians 14:18). Every Spirit-filled believer should use this gift regularly in private prayer.

The gift of diverse tongues, on the other hand, is meant for a public setting, such as a church service or group gathering. It's when someone delivers a message in tongues aloud, and it requires interpretation so the body can be edified.

Paul laid out this distinction clearly in 1 Corinthians 14:2 and 14:5:

> "For he who speaks in a tongue does not speak to men but to God, for no one understands him…"

> "I wish you all spoke with tongues, but even more that you prophesied; for he who prophesies is greater than he who speaks with tongues, unless indeed he interprets, that the church may receive edification."

Private tongues edify *you*. Public tongues edify the *church*. Both are valuable—but they function differently.

How the Gift of Interpretation of Tongues Operates

When someone receives a message from the Holy Spirit in tongues during a gathering, it should be delivered reverently, clearly, and boldly—not shouted over the preacher or used to interrupt the flow of the service. The Spirit of the prophet is subject to the prophet (1 Corinthians 14:32). This gift operates in order, not chaos.

The message must then be interpreted, either by the person who delivered it or by someone else who is gifted in interpretation. This is not translation, it's interpretation. The Spirit conveys the meaning.

When properly used, this gift causes the room to pause, listen, and receive a word directly from God in a way that carries weight, clarity, and an undeniable sense of God's presence.

Paul encouraged this gift, with proper boundaries: "If anyone speaks in a tongue, let there be two or at the most three, each in turn, and let one interpret" (1 Cor. 14:27). This helps protect the gathering from disorder or confusion, and it ensures that everything said brings strength to the church.

Why This Gift Matters

In a world filled with noise, opinions, and shallow speech, the gift of tongues reminds us that God speaks in a language the mind can't control. It's a sign that the Spirit is present—not just to stir emotion, but to release a divine message.

It also requires faith. When you speak out in tongues, you don't know what you're saying—you have to trust the Holy Spirit. That act of faith opens the door for God to do something unusual, unexpected, and powerful.

Some may be tempted to avoid this gift because it seems uncomfortable or unfamiliar. But remember—Paul didn't tell the Church to reject it. He told them to use it with maturity. 1 Corinthians 14:39: "Do not forbid to speak with tongues."

When this gift is silenced in the name of "relevance" or "comfort," something critical is lost. The Church loses a conduit through which God wants to speak. We don't need less supernatural; we need more order *in the supernatural*.

Personal Example

There was a powerful service one night, and a wave of deep intercession swept through the church. Suddenly, someone began to speak out in tongues—loud and clear, with a boldness that made everyone pause. I felt the unction to interpret. As I opened my mouth, the Spirit gave me the words: *"I am walking through this house, healing hearts and restoring callings. What was buried is being resurrected."* A woman in the back collapsed in tears. After service, she told me she had told God that morning, "If You don't speak to me tonight, I'm walking away." That's the power of this gift—it's not random. It's precise. It speaks directly to the soul.

Final Thoughts

The gift of tongues, when used in public, is never for show. It is sacred. It's a moment where heaven touches earth and the Spirit bypasses the mind to speak directly to the heart of the Church. It must be used with care. With humility. With submission to leadership. But it should not be neglected.

If you've been filled with the Holy Spirit, ask God to use you in this gift. Don't be afraid to yield when you feel that nudge. Speak when prompted. And trust that the same Spirit who gives the utterance will also give the interpretation.

This is not emotionalism. This is divine communication. Let the Spirit speak—even if the language is unknown.

Gift of Interpretation of Tongues

The gift of interpretation of tongues is a supernatural ability given by the Holy Spirit to interpret a message spoken in an unknown, heavenly language into a language the listeners can understand. It's not a translation in the natural sense—it's divine interpretation, inspired by the Spirit, so that the Church can be edified, comforted, and instructed. The Apostle Paul emphasized the importance of this gift in 1 Corinthians 14, making it clear that whenever tongues are spoken publicly in a gathering of believers, there should also be an interpretation so that the message is not left as a mystery. This gift acts as a bridge between the unseen utterance of the Spirit and the understanding of the Body, ensuring that God's voice is not only heard but also understood.

When Heaven Speaks, Understanding Must Follow

If the gift of diverse kinds of tongues is heaven's language, then the gift of interpretation is the unveiling of heaven's message into a form that the Church can understand. It is how the mysterious becomes clear, how the unknown becomes known, and how the Church is edified through supernatural communication. Paul made it clear in 1 Corinthians 14:13:

"Therefore let him who speaks in a tongue
pray that he may interpret."

This gift is not about natural linguistics—it's not someone who knows Spanish interpreting someone who speaks Portuguese. This is a spiritual gift that functions by revelation, not by education. The interpretation of tongues is how God ensures the body understands what the Spirit is saying when a message is delivered in an unknown tongue.

Not a Word-for-Word Translation

One of the most important things to understand is that interpretation is not translation. When God gives someone the gift of interpretation, they are not delivering a word-for-word decoding of what was spoken in tongues. They are capturing the essence, the burden, and the intent of the Spirit's message. The interpretation might be longer or shorter than the original utterance. That doesn't mean it's off—it just means it's Spirit-given insight, not academic translation.

1 Corinthians 14:27–28 puts it plainly:

> "If anyone speaks in a tongue, let there be two or at the most three, each in turn, and let one interpret. But if there is no interpreter, let him keep silent in church…"

Why? Because without interpretation, there is no edification. It becomes a moment of mystery without clarity—and God is not the author of confusion.

A Call to Clarity, Not Performance

The interpretation of tongues should never become a performance. It's not about theatrical tone or drawing attention to yourself. The power is not in the drama; the power is in the accuracy.

Interpretation should come with reverence. Clarity. Humility. When the Spirit gives the interpretation, it will always align with the Word of God. It will bring edification, encouragement, or correction. It will bear witness with the Spirit of the church leadership. This is why interpretation, like all gifts, should be submitted to the authority of the house. Even if you "feel" something, it should be checked and weighed. God works through order.

1 Corinthians 14:29 says: "Let two or three prophets speak, and let the others judge." That principle applies here too. Gifts don't exempt us from accountability—they call us to it.

Can You Interpret Your Own Tongues?

Yes—and often, you should. 1 Corinthians 14:13 says: "Let him who speaks in a tongue pray that he may interpret."

Sometimes, the same person who delivers the tongue will also receive the interpretation. It might come immediately, or it may require a moment of stillness and waiting. Either way, this kind of flow requires maturity and trust in the Spirit's timing. But whether it's the same person or someone else, the goal remains the same: that the Body may be edified (1 Cor. 14:5).

How to Grow in This Gift

Just like other gifts, the interpretation of tongues grows with use.

- Spend time in prayer and worship, asking the Lord to make your spirit more sensitive.
- If you feel an interpretation stirring but aren't sure, ask God for clarity before speaking.
- Submit your interpretation to spiritual covering. Let your leaders help you grow in accuracy.
- Don't be afraid to step out—but don't force it either. Interpretation flows. It doesn't need to be fabricated.

One of the best ways to develop this gift is by spending time in the Word. The more you know Scripture, the more you'll recognize if what you're feeling aligns with God's voice. You'll also begin to discern when something is *off*—and that's just as important.

Final Thoughts

The gift of interpretation of tongues is a beautiful bridge—from mystery to meaning, from heaven's utterance to the Church's understanding. We should never downplay it or avoid it. When done properly, it creates a holy pause—a moment where we all listen, not to man, but to the Spirit of God.

If you've ever felt stirred while someone else was speaking in tongues, pause and ask, *Lord, is that for me to interpret?* And if He gives you the word, speak it—not for attention, but for obedience. Because every time you step out in faith, the gifts grow. And when the Body hears the voice of the Spirit through tongues and interpretation—it hears the voice of God, loud and clear.

Guidelines for Order in the Church

The Gifts of the Spirit are powerful, but they must also be governed. Power without order leads to confusion. And confusion is never the fruit of the Holy Spirit.

Paul dealt with this very issue in the Corinthian church. They had the gifts. They had the zeal, but they also had chaos. People were shouting over each other, speaking in tongues with no interpretation, and claiming revelation without accountability. Instead of edification, their gatherings became spiritual chaos.

So, Paul, under the inspiration of the Holy Spirit, wrote these words:

"Let all things be done decently and in order"

(1 Corinthians 14:40).

This verse is often quoted in conservative circles to shut down spiritual expression. But notice what it says: Let all things be done. That's permission for the gifts to operate. *Then* it says—in order. That's the structure.

We need both freedom and order. Expression and accountability. Fire and foundation.

Let's break down the biblical guidelines Paul gives for how the gifts—especially the vocal gifts—are to operate in the church.

One at a Time

"If anyone speaks in a tongue, let there be two
or at the most three, each in turn, and let one
interpret."
—1 Corinthians 14:27

The first principle is simple: Don't all speak at once. When God gives a message in tongues, it should be delivered one at a time—not in competition, not in chaos, but in turn.

In a Spirit-filled service, it's common to feel a strong flow of tongues in the atmosphere. That may be for personal edification (praying in the Spirit), or it may shift into a public message. If it's public, someone must interpret. But even in that moment, Paul says there should be no more than two or three messages, and each must come in turn. This creates room for clarity. It helps the Body discern what God is saying. And it teaches self-control, because the Holy Spirit doesn't override your will. You can wait your turn.

Interpretation Must Follow

Paul says clearly: If there's no interpretation, the tongue should not be released publicly.

"But if there is no interpreter, let him keep
silent in church, and let him speak to himself
and to God" (1 Corinthians 14:28).

This doesn't mean you're forbidden to pray in tongues personally—it means that when you're in a corporate setting, you don't release a public message unless there's someone there to interpret. This protects the Body from confusion and ensures that every gift brings edification.

Now, this also means churches should teach and train people to interpret. The gift doesn't always mean a word-for-word decoding. It's not a spiritual Google Translate. It's an interpretation—a Spirit-led sense of what the message means. Sometimes it's shorter than the original tongue. Sometimes it's longer. But when it's right, the Body will know. There will be confirmation. Peace. Clarity.

Let the Prophets Speak—and Let Others Judge

> "Let two or three prophets speak, and let the others judge" (1 Corinthians 14:29).

Paul transitions here to prophecy—another vocal gift. The pattern is the same: a few at a time, and then let others judge. This is key. No one is above accountability. Even prophetic words must be tested—not by feelings, but by the Word of God and by mature spiritual leadership. If a prophetic word cannot be judged, it shouldn't be delivered. Period.

Prophets don't just declare—they submit. And when the Church has a healthy culture of prophecy, people feel safe, not suspicious. They know the word has been weighed.

The Spirits of the Prophets Are Subject to the Prophets

> "And the spirits of the prophets are subject to the prophets. For God is not the author of confusion but of peace..." (1 Corinthians 14:32–33)

This is a critical verse. It means that even in the strongest prophetic flow, the speaker is still in control. You can pause. You can wait. You can submit it to leadership. You are never "overtaken" by the Holy Spirit to the point of disorder.

Anytime someone says, *I couldn't help it—I just had to release that word*, it should raise a red flag. God's Spirit doesn't work like that. He moves through willing vessels, not possessed ones. Order doesn't quench the Spirit, it honors Him. When the Spirit is honored, the gifts flow even more freely.

Let All Things Be Done… In Order

We must get this deep into our spirit: The goal of spiritual gifts is edification, not exhibition. The goal is for the Church to be built up—not for individuals to be seen.

When services get out of order, when tongues erupt with no interpretation, when prophecy becomes performance, when people shout over each other, the result isn't glory. It's confusion. That's why Paul ends 1 Corinthians 14 with this:

"Let all things be done decently and in order."
(v. 40)

Not all things except the gifts. Not all things except the spontaneous. All things done in order.

Order and Fire Can Coexist

A lot of people fear that if we put guidelines on the gifts, we'll shut them down. However, it's the opposite. Order creates space for fire to burn without destroying the house. It channels the flow of the Spirit into something powerful, consistent, and transformative.

Think of it like electricity. Uncontained, it's dangerous. But when wired properly, it lights up a whole city. That's what the gifts are meant to do: light up the

Church, not confuse it. Not divide it. Not hijack it. But empower it, build it, and unify it under the Lordship of Jesus Christ. So let the gifts flow, but let them flow in order.

CHAPTER 7

Spiritual Impartation and Growth

You weren't meant to stay where you started. The Gifts of the Spirit aren't static. They grow. They mature. They deepen as you walk with God. Just like muscles respond to resistance and seeds respond to water, the gifts in you respond to hunger, obedience, and exposure to the anointing.

There's something else that accelerates spiritual growth—something that can't be manufactured, but it can be received: impartation.

Throughout Scripture, we see moments where power was passed. Where mantles were transferred. Where gifts were stirred. Not just by being present, but through an encounter. Through relationship. Through laying on of hands. Through submission to spiritual authority.

Impartation isn't magic. It's not personality. It's not hype. It's the Holy Spirit honoring spiritual lineage—flowing through one vessel to awaken something in another. And when you receive impartation in the right spirit, it doesn't just stir your gift—it anchors your growth. This final section is all about how to grow in what God has already given you. How to guard it. How to stir it. How to walk with maturity, so you don't just burn bright for a moment, but instead you burn consistently for a lifetime.

How Spiritual Impartation Happens

Spiritual gifts don't begin with people—they begin with God. Throughout Scripture, we see that God often uses people to activate what He's already placed inside someone else. That's called impartation.

Paul writes in Romans 1:11:

"For I long to see you, that I may impart to you some spiritual gift, so that you may be established."

He doesn't say "teach you" or "preach to you"—he says impart. That word means to transfer, to release, to deposit something spiritual from one vessel into another. So how does impartation happen?

Impartation Through the Laying On of Hands

Paul told Timothy in 2 Timothy 1:6:

> "Therefore I remind you to stir up the gift of God which is in you through the laying on of my hands."

Laying on of hands isn't just symbolic—it's spiritual. It's a biblical method of transferring authority, anointing, and gifting. When done under proper authority and in a holy atmosphere, it becomes a moment where heaven touches earth.

Impartation through hands must be done with discernment. It's not a light thing. You don't let just anyone lay hands on you—and you don't lay hands on someone without spiritual responsibility. There must be relationship. There must be alignment. There must be reverence. But when the moment is right—when the vessel is ready—something supernatural can be activated.

Impartation Through Prophetic Declaration

Sometimes, impartation comes through the spoken word. A prophetic word can call out what's dormant. It can awaken a gift that's been sleeping. It can launch someone into a level of spiritual boldness they didn't know was possible. We see this all throughout the Bible—from Elijah declaring a double portion to Elisha, to Jesus speaking destiny over Peter, to Paul releasing assignments over young leaders. Words carry weight—especially when they're Spirit-breathed.

If you've ever had someone speak over you and something inside of you shifted—that's impartation at work.

Impartation Through Proximity to the Anointing

This might be the most overlooked, but it's just as powerful: you receive by who you walk with. Elisha followed Elijah for years. He didn't just show up for the mantle, he served the man. And when Elijah was taken up, Elisha didn't inherit his charisma, he inherited his calling.

Sometimes impartation comes not by what's taught, but by what's caught. The more you stay close to the anointing, the more you begin to walk in it. You learn the patterns. You absorb the flow. You receive without even realizing it.

Impartation Through Honor and Hunger

There's no impartation without honor. You can't receive from someone you secretly resent. You can't grow under someone you refuse to submit to. Honor unlocks what they carry. And when honor is mixed with hunger—something powerful happens.

This isn't about idolizing people. It's about recognizing what God has placed in them and saying, "I want to grow from that." It's about respecting the oil they carry—and being willing to pay the price to carry your own.

Final Thoughts

Impartation doesn't make you someone else—it awakens who God created you to be. And once it's received, your job is to steward it well. Stir it up. Protect it. Pray into it. Use it. Because impartation is never just for you—it's so you can pour into others.

Just like someone laid hands on you—one day, you'll lay hands on the next generation. So, stay humble, stay hungry, and let the fire keep growing.

Staying Close to the Anointing

If you want to walk in power, you've got to stay close to the fire.

There's a principle I've learned over the years—I call it the *eye-contact principle*. In the Kingdom of God, impartation is often less about information and more about proximity. Yes, you can read books, watch sermons online, and attend conferences, however, there are some things you can only receive by walking closely with someone who carries the anointing.

Think about Elisha. He wasn't known for preaching great messages. He didn't have a big following. He was simply faithful to follow Elijah. He was there through the highs and the lows. He saw the miracles, but he also saw the moments when nobody else was watching. He wasn't after fame—he was after what Elijah carried. And when the moment came—when the chariots of fire arrived to take Elijah home—Elisha didn't just cry. He reached for the mantle.

> "And Elisha saw it, and he cried out, 'My father, my father, the chariot of Israel and its horsemen!' So he saw him no more. And he took hold of his own clothes and tore them in two pieces. He also took up the mantle of Elijah…" (2 Kings 2:12–13).

Here's the part we miss: Elisha only caught the mantle because he was close enough to see it fall.

Proximity Precedes Power

You can't receive from afar what God intended to be passed up close.

We live in a digital age and thank God for it, but YouTube clips don't carry impartation. Podcasts won't pass the mantle. You have to *walk with* someone. Serve beside them. Ask questions. Sit in their shadow. Watch how they pray, how they listen, how they lead. And little by little, something begins to transfer.

When people are around the gift, the gift begins to reproduce itself. You begin to impart what is in your spirit to others. This is why it's so important to stay close to people who flow in the Spirit. Not just to admire their gift, but to catch the atmosphere they carry. Gifts multiply in healthy environments. And when you're around someone who walks in sensitivity and boldness, that same boldness begins to stir in you.

This is how I learned to flow in the Spirit. I didn't just read books on the gifts—I got around people who walked in them. I watched how my mentors would listen for the voice of God. I'd see them pause mid-service, shift the whole atmosphere, and obey the Spirit—even when it didn't make sense. I would ask questions. I'd stay late. I'd carry their bags. I just wanted to be around the anointing. Not to be seen. Not to be next. Just to learn.

The Mantle Can't Be Microwaved

Some of the most powerful moments in my life didn't come from being on a stage—they came from being *in the room*. There were moments when a man of God would speak into my life—and something would shift. Not because I earned it. Not because I was talented, but because I *stayed close*.

And here's the thing: most people miss it because they leave too soon. They grow impatient. They want their own platform. They think they're ready before they've been proven. But Elisha stayed all the way to the end. Even when Elijah told him to stay behind, Elisha said, "As the Lord lives and as your soul lives, I will not leave you" (2

Kings 2:6). That's the posture of someone who's ready to carry the mantle: unwavering faithfulness.

Spiritual Fathers and Covering

You were never meant to walk alone. The biblical pattern has always been mentorship, covering, and lineage. Paul had Timothy. Moses had Joshua. Naomi had Ruth. Elijah had Elisha. Jesus had the disciples.

Who are you walking with? Who speaks into your life—not just to cheer you on, but to correct you, to shape you, to challenge you?

Covering isn't control. It's protection. It's the fence that lets you run with freedom, without falling off the cliff. And when you stay submitted—when you stay planted—the oil that flows from the head begins to reach you too.

"It is like the precious oil upon the head, running down on the beard, the beard of Aaron, running down on the edge of his garments" (Psalm 133:2).

That's impartation through alignment. The flow starts at the top, but it reaches those who stay connected.

Final Thoughts

You don't chase the anointing—you stay close to it. You don't demand a mantle—you receive it through faithfulness. And when the time is right, God will make sure you're in position to catch what's falling.

So, if you're reading this and wondering, *how do I grow in the gifts? How do I get to that next level?*—let me ask you this: Whose footsteps are you following? Because if you stay close to the anointing, eventually, the oil will find you.

Ministering in the Moment: Flowing with the Holy Spirit During Altar Calls and Services

The altar is not just a closing tradition. It's not just the "emotional part" of a church service. It is the moment where heaven often touches earth. It's where burdens are lifted. Where chains break. Where clarity comes. And for many people, it's the place where they hear God clearly for the very first time.

But here's the truth: if we don't know how to minister in the moment—if we're not trained to flow with the Holy Spirit when He starts moving—then we'll miss what God wants to do in those sacred windows.

The Altar Is a Place of Flow, Not Formula

You can't approach altar ministry like a checklist. The same method won't work every time. Jesus never healed the same way twice. One moment He spoke. The next, He touched. Another time He made mud and told someone to go wash. Why? Because it wasn't about the method—it was about obedience to the Spirit in the moment.

We must train ourselves to respond, not react. To listen, not just perform. That's what it means to minister in the moment.

Learning to Read the Room

Sometimes the Spirit will fall heavy—people weep, fall on their knees, and nothing needs to be said. Don't interrupt that moment just because the program says it's time for a closing song. Let God be God.

Other times, there's a resistance in the room. That's when you lean into the Spirit. It's not about forcing something, it's about discerning what heaven wants to release and aligning yourself with it.

I remember being in a service where nothing was moving. The worship was good. The preaching was solid. But there was a wall in the Spirit. I asked the Lord, "What do You want to do right now?" And the Lord said, *"Break the spirit of heaviness with praise."* So, I got up and began to lead a shout of praise—not emotional hype, but prophetic praise. And when the people responded, the atmosphere cracked wide open. People who had come in bound were suddenly being delivered. That's the power of ministering in the moment.

Don't Be Afraid to Wait

One of the most powerful things you can do in altar ministry is wait. Don't rush. Don't fill the silence with noise. Sometimes, it's in the stillness that the Spirit speaks most clearly.

In 1 Kings 19, God didn't speak to Elijah through the wind, the earthquake, or the fire. He spoke through a still small voice. That same voice is speaking in your services. Will you hear it? Will you respond?

Ask, Listen, Obey

When ministering to someone in an altar moment, don't start with what you *think*. Start with what you *hear*. Ask the Lord:

"God, what are You doing in this person right now?"

"How should I pray?"

"What should I say—or not say?"

Sometimes, the Lord may show you something very specific—a word of knowledge, a phrase, or even a picture. Sometimes, He'll just give you a burden. Follow the prompting, not your preference. And don't be afraid of silence. Lay your hand on them (when appropriate), and just wait. The Holy Spirit doesn't need your words to move. God just needs your obedience.

Flowing as a Team

If you're leading altar workers, teach them to flow together. Don't all rush to pray over the same person. Don't get competitive. Don't dominate the moment with loud praying if God is moving quietly.

It's not about who has the best prayer. It's about *yielding* to the flow. If someone is already praying for a person, ask the Lord if you're supposed to join them—or just agree quietly. Sometimes, your role is to intercede a few feet away.

Unity at the altar is powerful. And when the team is aligned in the Spirit, the results are undeniable.

Sensitivity, Not Spectacle

We're not there to put on a show. Altar ministry is not a stage. It's a delivery room—where new things are birthed in the Spirit. Don't try to make something happen just because the crowd is watching. Don't try to recreate a past moment. Be present. Be available. And let God lead.

What to Do After the Moment

After the breakthrough, after the prophecy, after the tears—what next? Encourage the person to *seal it*. To give God thanks. To stay in prayer. Sometimes, even to write it down. And when appropriate, follow up. Altar ministry doesn't end at the altar—it often begins there.

Let the Spirit Lead

Ministering in the moment takes courage. It takes discernment. But more than anything, it takes surrender. You don't need the perfect words. You just need a sensitive spirit and a willing heart. If you walk into the altar with that posture—God will use you. Again, and again.

The altar is not a stage. It's a sacred place and you were born to minister in it.

Stirring Up the Gift

There's something inside of you, something God placed there on purpose, and it's time to stir it up.

Paul's words to Timothy were not just encouragement; they were a divine charge:

"Therefore I remind you to stir up the gift of God which is in you through the laying on of my hands" (2 Timothy 1:6).

That word *"stir"* means to rekindle a flame. To agitate the embers. To fan it back to life. Which tells us something important: the gift can lie dormant if left unattended.

The Gift is There… But Is It Moving?

You don't have to chase after something new—you already carry something powerful. But gifts don't operate on autopilot. They require engagement. They require faith. They require a response. You can be filled with the Holy Ghost, called by God, gifted by the Spirit—and still not walk in the fullness of what's available to you. Not because you're disqualified, but because you haven't stirred it.

We stir the gifts of the Spirit through prayer. Through fasting. Through obedience to even the smallest whisper of the Spirit. Every act of obedience adds oxygen to the flame.

We stir the gifts when we step out in faith, even when we feel unsure. When we lay hands on someone and believe for healing. When we open our mouth to speak the word God gave us, even if our voice shakes. Stirring is not a feeling, it's an action.

Don't Wait for Permission

Some people spend their whole lives waiting: Waiting for someone to call them up. Waiting for a mic. Waiting for someone to recognize what's in them. But Paul didn't say, "Wait until others stir your gift." He said, "Stir up the gift of God which is in you." (2 Timothy 1:6).

That means the responsibility is yours. The gift was given to you by God, but the flame is your job to keep burning. Yes, submission matters. Yes, spiritual authority matters. But don't confuse humility with hesitation. Stirring your gift doesn't mean self-promotion—it means being faithful. Being bold. Saying yes to God when He prompts you.

When You Stir It, God Multiplies It

Gifts don't grow through neglect. They grow through use. The more you stir, the stronger it becomes. The more you obey, the more authority you walk in. And something powerful happens when you take the first step: God breathes on it.

Just like the widow in 2 Kings 4 had to start pouring oil for the multiplication to happen—you have to start moving for the anointing to flow. The miracle didn't come when she *waited*. It came when she *poured*.

A Church Full of Stirred Gifts

Can you imagine what the Church would look like if every believer stirred up the gift inside them? What would happen if every youth, every elder, every woman and man began to walk boldly in what God had deposited? What would happen if we stopped waiting for someone else to do it—and we stirred what's already in our hands?

This generation doesn't need another celebrity preacher. It needs a Body that's fully alive. Fully awakened. Fully activated. And it starts with a decision: No more passive faith. No more buried gifts. No more waiting for the "right time." Now is the time. Stir it up.

Avoiding the Counterfeit and Standing Through Criticism

Wherever there is something real, the enemy will always try to produce a copy. And the more powerful and precious a thing is, the more fiercely it will be imitated.

That's why we must talk about this: not just how to pursue the gifts, but how to guard them. Because for every true move of the Spirit, there's a counterfeit version trying to deceive, distract, and discredit the work of God.

Paul warned the Corinthian church—a church full of spiritual gifts—not to be ignorant of spiritual things. Why? Because immaturity mixed with power is dangerous. When people are hungrier for *manifestations* than they are for *truth*, they become easy targets for deception.

"Beloved, do not believe every spirit, but test the spirits, whether they are of God…" (1 John 4:1).

The Counterfeit is Loud, Flashy, and Self-Centered

The true gifts of the Spirit are rooted in love, humility, and obedience. They point people to Jesus, not to the person being used. But the counterfeit is always trying to steal the spotlight. The counterfeit says, "Look at me." The authentic gift says, "Listen to Him."

The counterfeit stirs emotion without transformation. It performs without fruit. It may look powerful, but it leaves people unchanged.

You can shout. You can prophesy. You can even mimic tongues. But if there's no fruit, no humility, and no alignment with Scripture, it's not the Holy Ghost. The Spirit of God does not operate outside of the Word of God. That's how we test the gift: By the Word. By the fruit. By the posture of the vessel.

Simon the Sorcerer Wanted the Power… Without the Process

In Acts 8, we read about a man named Simon who practiced sorcery in Samaria. He amazed people with his "power"—so much so that people believed he was operating in the power of God. But when Simon saw the apostles lay hands and people receive the Holy Ghost, he offered them money. He wanted access, but not accountability. He wanted the power, but not the relationship. Peter rebuked him sharply: "Your money perish with you, because you thought that the gift of God could be purchased with money!" (Acts 8:20).

That's the spirit of the counterfeit: trying to *buy* what can only be birthed. Trying to *perform* what must be carried. Gifts don't come through ambition. They come through intimacy. Through prayer. Through fasting. Through death to self. That's why some people are talented but powerless—because they've skipped the altar.

Guard Your Hunger

The enemy preys on the hungry. If you're desperate for spiritual things, that's good—but don't let desperation blind you to deception. You must discern. Be humble enough to learn. Stay rooted in the Word. Stay submitted to your leaders. Ask the hard questions. Don't chase the dramatic—chase the authentic.

And if something doesn't feel right in your spirit, don't ignore it. Don't override the check in your heart just because someone has a big platform or a loud voice. The Holy Spirit leads with peace, not pressure.

Stay Grounded in Holiness

There's no shortcut to the gifts. No formula. No secret code. The gifts flow through a life of holiness, a life of prayer, and a heart that says yes to God, even when no one's watching.

If you want to walk in real power—the kind that changes lives, the kind that breaks chains—you have to stay rooted. Grounded. Hidden in Him.

If the devil can't stop you with fear, he'll try to push you with pride. If he can't silence you with doubt, he'll distract you with hype. That's why every gift must stay submitted. Every anointing must stay accountable and every ministry must stay surrendered.

Let the Fire Be Pure

God is raising up a people who don't just want fire—they want pure fire. Not strange fire. Not man-made fire. Not counterfeit fire. But the kind of fire that comes from the altar—the kind that purifies and empowers at the same time.

The Holy Ghost is real. The gifts are real. But so is the counterfeit. So don't just ask, "Is it powerful?" Ask, "Is it pure?" Don't just ask, "Did it move people?" Ask, "Did it glorify Jesus?" Don't just ask, "Is it anointed?" Ask, "Is it accountable?"

Let your hunger lead you to the feet of Jesus, not into spiritual performance. Stay low. Stay clean. Stay submitted. And the real gifts will not only flow through you—they'll multiply through you.

Facing Criticism Without Losing Confidence

If you're going to operate in the gifts of the Spirit, criticism is inevitable. You'll be misunderstood. You'll be misquoted. You'll be labeled "emotional," "unbalanced," or "doing too much." Sometimes the resistance comes from skeptics who don't believe in miracles. Other times, it comes from believers who have been wounded by spiritual abuse, or simply don't understand how the gifts work.

Even Jesus wasn't exempt. In Matthew 12, when He cast out a demon, the Pharisees accused Him of doing it by the power of Satan. That's right, Jesus Himself was accused of being demonic. If they questioned Him, they'll question you too.

Paul faced it. He told the Corinthians, "With me it is a very small thing that I should be judged by you or by a human court. ... He who judges me is the Lord" (1 Corinthians 4:3–4). He understood that obedience to God would always invite resistance from man.

So, what do you do when the criticism comes?

1. Don't get defensive. Get discernment.

Not every critic is your enemy. Sometimes their concern comes from genuine confusion or past pain. Don't be quick to attack. Listen. Discern. And if there's truth in what they're saying, be humble enough to grow. But if it's just noise—move forward in peace.

2. Stay submitted to spiritual covering.

The safest people in the gifts are the ones who are under authority. When you're aligned with leadership, accusations lose their grip. You don't have to defend yourself—your fruit and your submission will speak for you.

3. Let fruit speak louder than fire.

You can shout. You can prophesy. You can stir the atmosphere. But if people don't see love, peace, consistency, and humility in your life, they'll tune you out. Long-term credibility comes through fruit, not just fire.

4. Keep your heart clean.

The moment criticism makes you bitter, it's no longer about the gifts—it's about pride. Shake the dust off your feet, forgive, and keep your spirit pure. Don't let offense block your flow.

5. Remember who you're doing this for.

You're not here to impress crowds. You're not here to prove something. You're here to obey God. If He says speak, speak. If He says wait, wait. If He says lay hands, do it in faith. Your audience is heaven, not the critics.

Criticism doesn't mean you're wrong—it often means you're effective. And when people can't explain your anointing, they'll try to control it. Stay teachable. Stay accountable. But don't stop flowing.

CHAPTER 8

The Fruit of the Spirit
Character That Carries the Gifts

The Apostle Paul describes the church as "built upon the foundation of the apostles and prophets, Jesus Christ Himself being the chief cornerstone" (Ephesians 2:20). The Fivefold Ministry establishes the foundation, and the gifts of the Spirit bring empowerment for service.

Yet there is another dimension without which the Church cannot remain steady: the fruit of the Spirit.

The gifts and the fruit are not in competition but in cooperation. Too often, believers emphasize one while neglecting the other. Some pursue the gifts with zeal but fail to cultivate the fruit. Others are careful to walk in holiness and character but shy away from spiritual gifts. Paul makes it plain that both are necessary. The gifts display the power of God; the fruit displays the character of Christ. The gifts flow through us, but the fruit grows within us. Together, they create the balance God intended.

Gifts Without Fruit

Paul lists nine gifts of the Spirit in 1 Corinthians 12: word of wisdom, word of knowledge, faith, gifts of healing, working of miracles, prophecy, discerning of spirits, tongues, and interpretation of tongues. These are supernatural abilities given by the Spirit for the common good, to edify the body of Christ and equip the Church for mission. Without the gifts, the Church lacks the power and effectiveness to carry out its calling.

Yet gifts alone are not enough. The Corinthian church operated freely in the gifts, yet Paul had to correct them because they were immature, carnal, and divided. Power without character becomes dangerous. Gifts without fruit can result in pride, misuse, or even spiritual abuse. Paul warned of this danger when he wrote: "Though I speak with the tongues of men and of angels, but have not love, I have become sounding brass or a clanging cymbal" (1 Corinthians 13:1). Gifts without fruit are nothing more than noise without lasting impact.

A prophetic word given without love may wound instead of edify. A miracle without humility may draw attention to the minister instead of Christ. A manifestation of tongues without self-control may cause confusion rather than blessing. Where the fruit is absent, the gifts become distorted, and the result is spiritual imbalance.

The Fruit of the Spirit

In contrast, Paul teaches in Galatians 5:22–23 that "the fruit of the Spirit is love, joy, peace, longsuffering, gentleness, goodness, faith, meekness, temperance: against such there is no law." Unlike the gifts, which are distributed differently to each believer as the Spirit wills, the fruit is expected in the life of every believer. No Christian is exempt from the call to bear fruit, because fruit is the evidence of the Spirit's inner work.

Jesus Himself declared, "By their fruit you shall know them" (Matthew 7:16). It is not gifts, but fruit, that reveals authenticity. Gifts may impress the crowd, but fruit proves the reality of a transformed life. The Spirit does not only want to manifest through us in power, but to form Christ within us in character.

This is why the fruit is essential. It demonstrates that the Spirit's work is not superficial but transformative. Love, joy, peace, patience, kindness, goodness, faithfulness, gentleness, and self-control anchor the believer so that power does not outpace maturity. The fruit of the Spirit is the anchor that keeps the gifts of the Spirit from drifting into misuse.

How the Fruit Governs the Gifts

The relationship between gifts and fruit is not abstract—it is practical and visible. Each gift, if left unchecked, can be misapplied. But when tempered by the fruit of the Spirit, gifts find their proper expression.

Love governs prophecy. Without love, a prophetic word may tear down; with love, it comforts, exhorts, and edifies (1 Corinthians 14:3).

Compassion governs healing. Jesus did not heal merely to prove power, but because He was moved with compassion (Matthew 14:14). Separating healing from compassion risks exalting the person ministering the healing rather than glorifying the Healer.

Self-control governs tongues. Paul reminded the Corinthians that the exercise of tongues must be done in order, with interpretation, so that all may be edified (1 Corinthians 14:27–28, 40). Without temperance, tongues become a source of confusion rather than a channel of worship.

Meekness governs wisdom. A word of wisdom or knowledge delivered in arrogance may crush those who hear it, but when spoken with gentleness, it brings life.

Patience governs faith. A gift of faith that is impatient may demand results on human terms, but when shaped by longsuffering, it remains steady, trusting in God's perfect timing.

In every case, the fruit of the Spirit ensures that the gifts of the Spirit are exercised in alignment with the heart of Christ. The gifts reveal what God can do through us; the fruit reveals who God is in us.

The Goal: Maturity in Christ

The balance of gifts and fruit leads us toward the ultimate goal of Christian life: maturity in Christ. Paul writes in Ephesians 4:13 that God has given gifts to the Church "till we all come to the unity of the faith and of the knowledge of the Son of God, to a perfect man, to the measure of the stature of the fullness of Christ." The gifts are tools to equip and build up the Body; the fruit is the evidence that Christ's nature is taking root within us.

Without the gifts, ministry lacks effectiveness. Without the fruit, ministry lacks authenticity. But when both operate together, the Church displays the fullness of Jesus Christ—His power and His character.

A Call to Pursue Both

Paul exhorts us in 1 Corinthians 14:1: "Pursue love, and desire spiritual gifts." Notice the order—love first, then gifts. Love, the first fruit of the Spirit, must govern every gift we operate in. When we pursue the fruit, the gifts flow in balance. When we pursue the gifts, we must do so under the guidance of the fruit.

The Church does not need to choose between power and character. It desperately needs both. Gifts without fruit may lead to imbalance, and fruit without gifts may lack power. But together they produce a mature, Spirit-filled witness that reveals Christ to the world.

The Spirit longs not only to empower the Church but to shape it into the likeness of Jesus. When His gifts and His fruit are in harmony, the Church becomes a living testimony of both His authority and His nature. That is the balance God designed.

CHAPTER 9

The Urgent Call

This is not a time for hesitation. This is a time for activation.

You've read the stories. You've seen the Scriptures. You've learned about the gifts of the Spirit, the order, the sensitivity, the flow. But none of it matters if it stays on the page. This moment—right now—is about *what you do next*.

Because the world is not waiting for another conference. The Church doesn't need another celebrity preacher. What God is looking for is a vessel—someone hungry, humble, and willing to say *yes*.

We are in a generation that is desperate for the real. Desperate for clarity in a time of confusion. Desperate for healing in a time of trauma. Desperate for discernment in a time of deception. And the answer is not just louder preaching. It's not just better branding. The answer is the power of the Holy Spirit flowing through everyday believers who are fully surrendered.

"The earnest expectation of the creation eagerly waits for the revealing of the sons of God" (Romans 8:19).

This generation is waiting for you to awaken.

You may have been on the sidelines. You may have been unsure. Maybe no one ever told you that you were called. But now you know. You've been filled with the Holy Spirit for a reason. You've been marked for a purpose. The same Spirit that raised Jesus from the dead is living inside of you—not just to comfort you, but to flow through you.

You don't need a platform to operate in the gifts. You don't need a pulpit to hear from God. What you need is a *yes*. A surrendered heart. A consistent prayer life. A posture of humility. And a willingness to walk in faith even when it feels uncomfortable.

I don't care what your background is. I don't care how broken your past has been. If God could use a young man from the streets of Compton—if He could pull me out of jail and addictions and place me in the middle of revival—then He can use you too. And not years from now. Not once you "have it all together." He wants to use you *now*.

Don't wait for someone else to do what you were born to do. Stir up the gift. Fan the flame. Step out in boldness. Because this world needs what God has placed inside of you.

This is not a suggestion. This is an urgent call.

Prophetic Prayer and Activation Moment

Right now, wherever you are—pause. Set this book down for a moment. Take a deep breath and pray this out loud:

"Lord Jesus, I surrender.
I give You my hands.
I give You my mind.
I give You my heart.
Stir up every gift You've placed inside of me.
I don't want to sit on the sidelines anymore.
I want to walk in Your power.
I want to move in Your Spirit.
I want to glorify You with everything I am.
So teach me to hear Your voice.
Fill me with boldness.
Burn away anything in me that blocks the flow.
And send me, Lord—wherever You want

me to go.

I say *yes*. In Jesus' name. Amen."

Now go live it. Let the fire fall. Let the gifts flow. Let heaven invade earth through you in the mighty name of Jesus!

Available in Spanish

Order at:
pastorjoeprado.com

www.ingramcontent.com/pod-product-compliance
Lightning Source LLC
Chambersburg PA
CBHW050909160426
43194CB00011B/2346